Sports Illustrated™

TIGER WOODS

CELEBRATING 25 YEARS ON THE PGA TOUR

CONTENTS

Tiger Woods at the 2007 Buick Invitational
at Torrey Pines in La Jolla, Calif.

Tiger's Tale

Twenty-five years ago golf's greatest prodigy
turned professional and embarked on a career
that has held fans spellbound

by BILL SYKEN

In an interview on CBS in the middle of February, Jim Nantz asked Tiger Woods a question that was completely straightforward but would seem oh so loaded a few days later: "Tiger, seven weeks from today, final round of the Masters. You going to be there?"
"God, I hope so," Tiger said, and then chuckled. "I have to get there first."

It was the chuckle of a man coming off his fifth back surgery, and who was 46 years old, coming up on the 25th anniversary of his turning pro. It was the chuckle of a man who had lived a career of unprecedented highs and surprising lows, and who knew that nothing was promised.

Days later, Tiger Woods was driving alone just before 7 a.m. in Rancho Palos Verdes near Los Angeles when he crashed his car in a single-vehicle accident. His Genesis GV80 SUV hit a tree, rolled over, and landed on its side. He sustained multiple fractures in his legs, and surgeons inserted a rod and pin and screws during emergency surgery.

The good news: The father of two survived a crash that could have easily been fatal. But the golf career of one of the great athletes of our time was in doubt.

Fans wondered, What should our expectations be?

With Tiger, that has been the question from the beginning.

The hype for Tiger began when he was not quite three years old, after he appeared on *The Mike Douglas Show* with a swing and a demeanor that were frighteningly advanced. As he grew into his teen years, he swept through youth and amateur championships as if he were truly a man among boys. His deeds alone would have created great anticipation about what Tiger Woods might accomplish as a professional. But then there was his father Earl, who had been guiding Tiger all along and who was the herald of all heralds. In 1996 Earl told SI writer Gary Smith, "Tiger will do more than any other man in history to change the course of humanity."

Earl's logic was: His son was possessed not just of talent, but of African, Asian, and Caucasian blood. He would connect to a global audience like no athlete had before. Therefore his son was uniquely qualified to deliver a message of change.

Tiger, remarkably, handled the load. He won his first professional major, the 1997 Masters, at age 21, by 12 strokes, and celebrated with an embrace of his father. Many more hugs followed as Tiger racked up the wins and ascended to the role of the most famous athlete on the planet, just as Earl predicted. One kink: It turned out Tiger's message to the world rarely went much deeper than "Buy a Buick." Although that's not entirely true, because really, the message was the winning itself.

Tiger's appearance on the global stage neatly overlapped with the exit of NBA superstar Michael Jordan, who concluded his "last dance" with the Chicago Bulls in 1998. Jordan was always the best point of comparison for him, more than Phil Mickelson or any of his PGA rivals could ever be. Woods was, like Jordan before him, the ultimate winner. Each in their red shirts, they came to personify what winning looked like, in a world where winning was becoming the greatest of all virtues. And Tiger provided one stunning example after another of how to do it.

Remember that chip at the 16th hole at Augusta?

Remember him fighting through pain at the 2008 U.S. Open?

Remember those four majors in a row?

Remember how, in 2019 at Augusta, he showed us all that he wasn't done yet?

Those performances, and dozens of others like them, were the true sum of his fist-pumping wisdom. And his Sunday sermons had the masses tuning in.

It's why, after his February SUV crash, players and fans showed up at the next tournament wearing Tiger's signature red shirt. At the time of his crash he was tied with Sam Snead for 82 career wins, the PGA Tour record. He has certainly given fans more than enough already. But if he can don the red shirt once more and come back and capture number 83, the roar would be heard around the world.

THIS BOOK is a celebration of both a career and a life. It's the story of one of the great athletes of our time, and it's also about a son becoming a father.

Because Tiger has been so good for so long, we have been able to watch him grow up. It has also meant that in the pages of SPORTS ILLUSTRATED, his story has been told by a breathtaking roster of writers, from golf specialists such as Alan Shipnuck, Michael Bamberger, and John Garrity to some of the most brilliant and decorated generalists in the history of the field: Gary Smith, Frank Deford, Rick Reilly, S.L. Price, Richard Hoffer, Steve Rushin, Michael Rosenberg. The same can be said of the photographers who haunted the fairways and greens, capturing the master at work.

SI devoted these resources to Tiger Woods because he is an essential figure in sports history, and the writing and photography in this collection does its best to rise up to the level of its subject. ●

Tiger competed in the
1995 NCAA Championship
in Columbus, Ohio.

Tiger celebrated his win at the 2005 Masters.

THE PRODIGY

Chapter 1

THROUGH 1996

Tiger played at Stanford from 1994 to '96, winning an NCAA individual title, before leaving college to join the PGA Tour.

YOUNG TIGER

YOUNG TIGER

At age two Tiger, accompanied by father Earl, made his TV debut, demonstrating his swing on *The Mike Douglas Show* on Oct. 6, 1978.

YOUNG TIGER

At age 15 Tiger, with Earl, tried to qualify for the 1991 Los Angeles Open; he would make the field in '92, becoming the youngest to play in a PGA event.

TIGER WOODS

YOUNG TIGER

Tiger celebrated
a birdie at the
17th hole at TPC
Sawgrass on his
way to a comeback
win at the 1994
U.S. Amateur.

Excerpted from SPORTS ILLUSTRATED, March 27, 2000

At 19, He Had the Golf World in Awe

From his earliest days Tiger Woods' parents trained their son so he could achieve the extraordinary

by RICK REILLY

When the boy was six, he asked his parents for the subliminal tape. In the parents' plan to raise the greatest golfer who ever lived, the boy's mind had to be trained. The tape was all rippling brooks and airy flutes on top and chest-thumpers underneath:

MY DECISIONS ARE STRONG! I DO IT ALL WITH MY HEART!

From the beginning, the boy understood what the tape was for, and he liked it. A regular Freud of the first grade. He would pop in the tape while swinging in front of the mirror or putting on the carpet or watching videos of old Masters tournaments. In fact, he played the tape so often that it would have driven any other parents quite nuts. Any other parents.

He took the messages that came with the tape and tacked them to the wooden bookshelf in his tiny room. All the people from *That's Incredible* and *Eye on L.A.* and *The Mike Douglas Show* who tracked in and out to meet the Great Black Hope, they all missed the messages. But there they were, right under their very ears.

I FOCUS AND GIVE IT MY ALL!

When the boy was seven, his parents installed the psychological armor. If he had a full wedge shot, the father would stand 15 feet in front of him and say, "I'm a tree." And the kid would have to hit over him. The father would jingle his change before the boy's bunker shots. Pump the brake on the cart on the boy's mid-irons. Rip the Velcro on his glove over a three-footer.

What his dad tried to do, whenever possible, was cheat, distract, harass and annoy him. You spend 20 years in the military, train with the Green Berets, do two tours of Nam and one of Thailand, you learn a few things about psychological warfare.

It was not good enough that by age two the boy could look at a grown man's swing and understand it ("Look, Daddy," he would say, "that man has a reverse pivot!"); that by three he was beating 10-year-olds; that by five he was signing autographs (because he couldn't write script, he printed his name in block letters); that by six he'd already had two holes in one. No, the father knew his son would need a mind as one-piece as his swing.

Let's see, the father would . . . drop a golf bag during the boy's backswing . . . roll a ball across the boy's line just before he putted . . . remind him not to snap-hook it there into the houses . . . jar him as he putted through . . . mark the father's own ball a foot closer to the hole than it was . . . make a 6 and write 5 . . . kick his own ball out of the rough, but only when his son was looking.

"I mean, yeah," says the boy now, "I'd get angry sometimes. But I knew it was for the betterment of me. That's what learning is all about, right?"

He was the father's one-boy battalion. Before tournaments the father would tell him to make sure his gear was in "tip-top shape, lie and loft." The father made sure the boy "understood the mission" (win). He would hold "debriefings" after the tournament (talk about how it went). What the father wanted for his son was the one thing he had had in battle, the thing that had kept Charlie from putting him in a bag: a "dark side," as he calls it, "a coldness." It was coldness that had allowed him to storm a VC-held village and step over dead men without swallowing hard. It had helped him to charge on against tracer fire without blinking when his every nerve screamed, "Get down!"

And so the boy learned coldness too. Eventually, nothing the father did could make him flinch. The boy who once heard subliminal messages under rippling brooks now couldn't hear a thing. Once at a tournament a marshal's walkie-talkie went off at volume 10 out of 10 during the boy's backswing. The boy admitted later that he never heard it.

"I wanted to make sure," says the father, "he'd never run into anybody who was tougher mentally than he was."

So far, the boy's USGA match-play record is 30-3.

MY WILL MOVES MOUNTAINS!

By second grade the boy had a nationally known name—Tiger Woods—and he had already played in, and won, his first international tournament, against kids from all over the world. His father took him to the 1st tee, where all the other nervous little boys and hyperventilating dads had gone. And he said, "Son, I want you to know I love you no matter how you do. Enjoy yourself." And then Tiger stepped up and hit a perfect drive. And after the round was over, the father asked him what he was thinking about as he stood over that first shot.

And Tiger said, simply, "Where I wanted my ball to go, Daddy."

Not: Don't miss it, don't skull it, don't fail.

Only: Where I wanted my ball to go.

"That's when I knew," says Earl Woods, the father. "That's when I knew how good he was going to be."

Since then, Tiger Woods has gone on to become exactly what his parents planned, the greatest golfer—at this stage of his life—ever to live. The little legend in the Coke-bottle glasses was so good that when he was 11 he went undefeated in Southern California junior golf events, some 30 tournaments in all, most with fields of more than 100 players. He was so overwhelming that golf deities bent knees to shake his hand. By his teens he had played with Sam Snead, been presented a tournament trophy by Lee Trevino, teed it up with Greg Norman, Jack Nicklaus and John Daly. He is the youngest person ever to have played in a PGA Tour event (at 16 years and two months, in the 1992 L.A. Open); the youngest ever and the first Black golfer to win the U.S. Amateur (last year, when he was 18, four years younger than Bobby Jones when he won his first Amateur, a year younger than Nicklaus when he won his); the first male ever to win three U.S. Juniors; the first male to win the Junior and the Amateur.

For a child to become a legend, his deeds must be legendary. Tiger Woods's were. His biggest victories all seemed snatched at the last second from other kids' trophy cases. Sure, he was the first boy to win three USGA Juniors, but look how he won them: in Orlando, on the 19th hole; in Milton, Mass., on the 18th; in Portland, on the 19th, after being two down with two to play and making two birdies—one on an unthinkable fairway bunker shot.

Before his greatest victory of all, in last year's U.S. Amateur on the Stadium course of the TPC at Sawgrass, his father whispered into his ear, "Let the legend grow." It practically doubled. Down six holes in the final match, Tiger roared murderously back, making two birdies in the last three holes—including a 139-yard wedge to the island-green 17th that stayed out of the water by three feet—to win 2 up. It's believed to be only the greatest comeback in the tournament's 99-year history.

"See, this is the first Black intuitive golfer ever raised in the United States," says Earl Woods. "Before, Black kids grew up with basketball or football or baseball from the time they could walk. The game became part of them from the beginning. But they always learned golf too late. Not Tiger. Ti-

ger knew how to swing a golf club before he could walk."

I BELIEVE IN ME!

From the beginning the idea was synergy: Produce a thing greater than the sum of its parts. But how? He and she were so opposite. He was 37. She was 23. He was a quarter American Indian, a quarter Chinese and half Black. She was half Thai, a quarter Chinese and a quarter white. He was from Manhattan, Kans. She was from Bangkok. He was a paid killer. She was a peaceful civilian. He was a Protestant. She was a Buddhist. He had raised himself. She came from a wealthy family. Both of his parents had died by the time he was 13. She still lived with hers.

Raise a wonder child? They could barely hook up for a first date. He was on assignment in Thailand, and she was working as a secretary in a U.S. Army office. He said eight, thinking p.m. She heard eight, thinking a.m. "Thai girls not go out at night," she says proudly. When she didn't show up, he figured she had stiffed him. When he didn't show up, she went and found him.

"We had a date," she sniffed. She was accompanied by a friend. ("Thai girls not go out unchaperoned," she says proudly.)

"Yeah," he said, his boots up on the desk. "Last night."

"We still have date," she said.

She insisted he take her to the temple of the Reclining Buddha, for it was a holy day in Bangkok. "What could I do?" growls Earl with a grin today. "I took her to the damn church."

They moved to Brooklyn, where they were married in 1969, and then to Cypress, Calif., where in 1975 she bore him a son, the First Son, in Asia the most important child, the one responsible for the family as soon as he's able. It was also her last child, since she suffered complications during the delivery. Together, the two of them, Earl and Tida, the two opposites, his yang to her yin, put all their love in one babbling, smiling, golf-swinging basket.

Maybe it's true: The hybrid rose is stronger than the two strains. They tended it as if it were the last rose in the garden. In his 18 years under their roof, Tiger never once had a baby-sitter. "I let my husband go," Tida says. "I stay with Tiger. Tiger more important than a party."

I WILL MY OWN DESTINY!

Even the name was part of the plan. Eldrick (Tiger) Woods. The "Eldrick" was made up out of the blue by Tida, because it joined the first letters of her husband's first name, Earl, and hers, Kultida. You understand? No matter what, we will always be there at your side.

The "Tiger" was given to him by his father in honor of his father's Vietnam combat partner, Nguyen Phong of the South Vietnamese army. Earl nicknamed Phong "Tiger" for his unblinking bravery. It was Tiger who took him on an insane mission through the streets of a VC-held village and got him the

Vietnamese silver star for it. It was Tiger, his best friend, who pulled him off a rice-paddy dike seconds after sniper fire tore over him. Around 1967 or '68 they lost contact, but Earl is convinced that Tiger is still alive somewhere in the world. And so he nicknamed his own son Tiger in hopes that someday Nguyen Phong would pick up a newspaper and read about Earl's famous son, the greatest golfer who ever lived, and understand.

IT HELPS ME UNCONSCIOUSLY!

When the boy was 13, they added the sports psychologist, Navy Capt. Jay Brunza, a family friend. He worked with Tiger the first time on a Saturday night—just some mind tricks, a little trance work—and then let Tiger join Brunza's little 12-man, low-bet choose-up. Tiger played two groups in front of Brunza, and halfway through the front nine an angry friend of Brunza's suddenly came trundling back in a cart. "What kind of monster have you created?" the man huffed. "He's birdied five of the first seven holes!"

The First Son is so clear-minded and open to all possibilities in golf that Brunza was able to hypnotize him in less than a minute. Once

" In his 18 years under their roof, Tiger never once had a baby-sitter. "I let my husband go," Tida says. "I stay with Tiger. Tiger more important than a party."

In 1995 Earl and Kultida Woods were already surrounded by their son's trophies.

he did it right in front of Earl without Earl's even knowing.

"Tiger, hold your arm out straight," Brunza said. Tiger did.

"Now, Earl, try to bend it." Earl pulled, pushed and even hung off that arm, and it wouldn't bend. Brunza got so good at hypno-

tizing Tiger, he could do it over the phone. Now, they are both so good at it, they don't have to do it at all.

Tiger can go into such deep levels of concentration that he doesn't even remember making shots. But the minds that most fascinate Brunza may be Earl's and Tida's. People sidle up to Brunza and whisper things like, "These two have got to have 'Little League Parents from Hell' written all over them, right?" But that's the thing: The Woodses break every stage-parent rule ever written. When dads drag their seven-year-olds up to Wayne Gretzky and say, "Wayne, will you tell him he's got to practice," Gretzky always says, "Nobody ever told me to practice." The same is true for Tiger Woods. Not once did Earl or Tida insist that he get in his golf practice. The trick was getting him home. Tiger's swing coach says that when Tiger and his dad come for sessions, Earl takes a chair and sits nearby, never saying a thing. "He not have to be Jack Nicklaus," Tida says of Tiger. "There too much pressure on the kid already." Says Earl: "If he should fail at this, we'll be his parachute. He'll land softly."

Ask the psychologist what would happen if Tiger suddenly said, "Mom. Pop. I'm selling my clubs. I'm taking up stamp collecting."

"Well," Brunza says, "I think they'd say, 'Great, Tiger. We're behind you 100 percent' and kiss him on the forehead."

I SMILE AT OBSTACLES!

When the Great Black Hope goes to the Augusta National Golf Club in two weeks as the most-anticipated young Black player to ever walk through its clubhouse doors, there will be only one weird thing.

He isn't Black.

Well, he is a quarter Black. But mostly he is Thai, and partly he is Chinese, and Tida wants you to know it. "All the media try to put Black in him," she says, rising off the couch. "Why don't they ask who half of Tiger is from? In United States, one little part Black is all Black. Nobody want to listen to me. I been trying to explain to people, but they don't understand. To say he is 100 percent Black is to deny his heritage. To deny his grandmother and grandfather. To deny me!"

Earl could argue that in this country, one-quarter Black is more than enough for

any racist. Earl should know. As the first Black baseball player in the history of the Big Eight Conference, back in the early 1950s (when it was the Big Seven), he was forced to stay in all-Black hotels apart from his white Kansas State teammates. He remembers all the times he heard other players on mostly white high school teams call him nigger. And he remembers the time when he was in a Little League tournament and the kid playing third base came up and said, accusingly, "Your skin is black." Earl said to the kid, "Lemme see your arm." And when the two of them turned the undersides of their forearms to the sky, Earl's was lighter than the flabbergasted boy's. Nobody tougher mentally.

But crusading is not part of the plan. The plan is for Tiger to knock down flags, not carry them. So Earl tells his son one rule: "When you're in America, be Black. When you're in the Orient, be Asian."

Come to think of it, Tiger might know a little about discrimination himself. Even as Tida carried him inside her, the little house in Cypress was pelted by limes and BB-gun fire from the Unwelcome Wagon, somebody who wasn't thrilled about the arrival of the first "Black" family in the neighborhood. On his first day of kindergarten Tiger was tied to a tree and taunted by older white kids. At 16 he received a death threat before playing in the L.A. Open at Riviera.

"I don't want to be the best Black golfer ever," he has said a hundred times. "I want to be the best golfer ever." But when he can fill in only one bubble under "Ethnicity" on forms? "I always fill in 'Asian,'" he says. He will be the fourth Black American to play in the Masters—in 61 years—but the first with a real chance to take home a green blazer someday. Lee Elder was 40 years old when he became the first Black golfer to play the Masters, in 1975. Calvin Peete played eight times, but his game was too short. Jim Thorpe (six times) never quite felt comfortable. None ever finished in the top 10.

But here, here is a kid of the '90s, too young to hate a club like Augusta National, a kid who considers himself of no real color, a kid with a future that is almost as huge as his dreams.

"My goal will be the same as always," Tiger says. "To learn something, enjoy myself and win." Still, he is ready for the questions when they come. "I know that I wouldn't be playing at Augusta if it weren't for what people like Charlie Sifford and Lee Elder did before me. They are pioneers. They are the Jackie Robinsons of golf."

MY STRENGTH IS GREAT!

At 16, when the boy had surpassed his father's knowledge, the father brought in the PGA Tour swing coach from Houston. Talk about pressure. Harmon, caretaker of Greg Norman's game, suddenly had Thomas Edison walk into his electronics school. The kid Tom Watson calls "the most important young golfer in the last 50 years" was Harmon's now, to either improve or entirely screw up.

Now Harmon can't get rid of the kid. "He wants to work with me 24 hours a day," the teacher says. "I can't get him off the phone."

Team Tiger says there's no way he'll leave school early and turn pro, unless, in his father's words, he "completely dominates" college golf his first three years. Then he may turn pro and play events in the summers and during Christmas and spring breaks while he finishes school. Uh, Professor Smithson? Can I get a makeup exam? I've got to play in this darn Skins Game. Of course, if you know Tida, you will bet on him turning pro only in time for the 1998 U.S. Open.

That doesn't mean Earl and Tiger can't start getting ready. Harmon has shortened

up Woods's backswing—a la Norman—and tightened up a few moving parts. And Tiger may hit the Tour as the most fit rookie in history. At 148 pounds, his bench-press rep is 215 pounds. On most days he works out a minimum of one hour on the weights, with another half an hour of aerobics and half an hour of stretching. Already, his bunker-rake body is starting to cut in. His biceps are outsized for his body, and his body fat is 5.5%. Stanford's former weight-room supervisor told golf coach Wally Goodwin that "pound for pound, Tiger's one of the strongest athletes on campus."

I AM FIRM IN MY RESOLVE!

At 18, he traded millions for a dorm room and no sleep.

Most any night you catch Tiger Woods and his roommate at Stanford, you'll notice Woods is not calling his agent, not getting a massage and not checking his investments. Usually, he is doing what his roomie is doing—cramming for a test and trying like hell to keep his hands off the TV remote, which, if it weren't for *The Simpsons*, he would have given up for the year. "No time," he says ruefully.

Many is the day when Tiger admits he'll be sitting in geophysics or art history class and thinking about what life would be if it weren't for all this damn character inside him. "Sometimes I'll be sitting there thinking, Dang, right now I'd be in Miami, getting ready for Doral, maybe playing a practice round with Greg Norman."

And when he is done daydreaming of courtesy cars and corporate cash, Tiger Woods climbs back up on his resolve. "Money won't make me happy," he says. "If I turned pro, I'd be giving up something I wanted to accomplish. And if I did turn pro, that would only put more pressure on me to play well, because I would have nothing to

> **"I don't want to be the best Black golfer ever," he has said a hundred times. "I want to be the best golfer ever."**

fall back on. I would rather spend four years here at Stanford and improve myself."

You say this guy is how old?

I FULFILL MY RESOLUTIONS POWERFULLY!

All they really wanted to give him was roots and wings. At 18, they let him go.

By March, Earl and Tida had not gone to visit Tiger at Stanford, not once, not for a tournament, not for anything.

Dozens and dozens of people have begged Earl and Tida to call their son and set up interviews, autograph sessions, favors, audiences and deals, but they have not interceded once. "It is time for him to have his own life now," says Tida.

Some days, though, it gets a little lonely. Tida will wander down the hall in the cozy little house in Cypress, into Tiger's cozy little bedroom, and see the words from the subliminal tape still tacked up on the bookshelf. Tida made up a résumé of Tiger's golf accomplishments—listed by age—and has a stack of copies sitting on the tiny computer table for visitors. Nearly every wall and nearly every table is crammed with Tiger tracks:

Tiger's awards, Tiger's photos, Tiger's trophies, hundreds and hundreds of them, swallowing the space from floor to ceiling, from window to door. But how will the great whole, the beautiful rose, do in a very big world without his two devoted gardeners?

Today some of the worst rainstorms of the past decade are pelting the Bay Area. There are floods and mud slides and even a few deaths. Earl and Tida are a little worried, especially because when they give the First Son a call, just to see if he's O.K., there's no answer.

No wonder. Tiger isn't somewhere safe. He is out here, alone, on the 10th hole of the closed Stanford golf course, in the middle of a horizontal wave of rain, his car the only one in the lot, and he is ripping two-irons into the teeth of an Auntie Em wind, getting ready for what he might face at St. Andrews. No coach ordered him here. No parent. No schedule. Hey, you don't get lucky and get this kind of horrible weather every day. Expect the best, prepare for the worst. And as the rain narrows his eyes and the gale wobbles his stance, you can't help noticing that he is smiling, a lifetime of subliminal messages happily at work. ●

1996 MASTERS

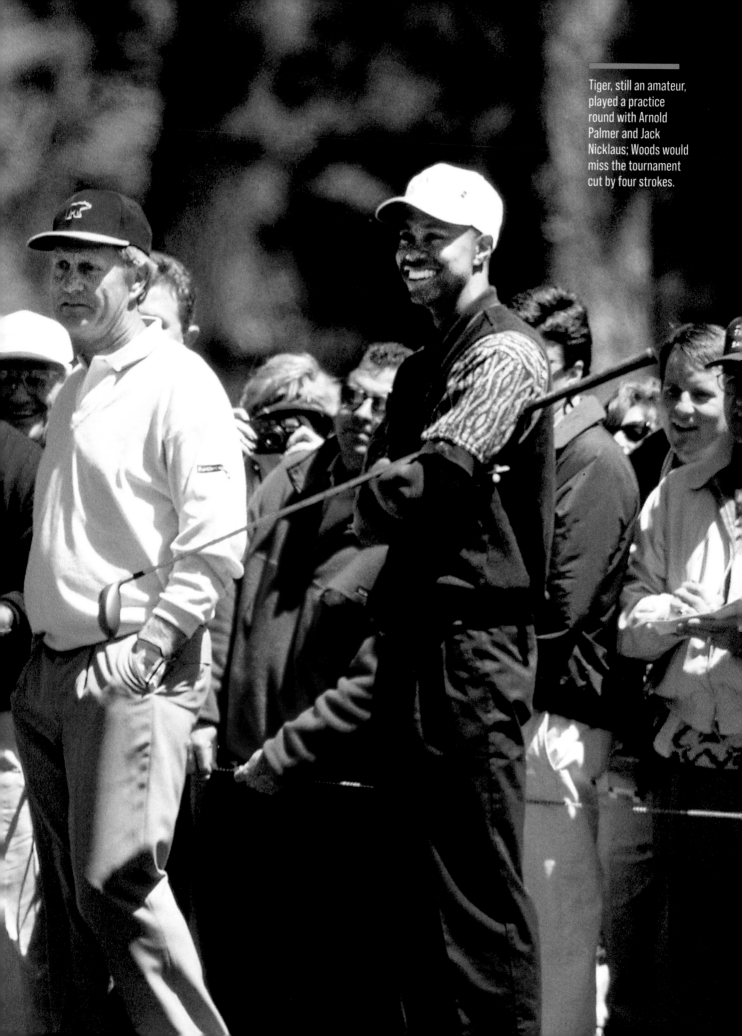

Tiger, still an amateur, played a practice round with Arnold Palmer and Jack Nicklaus; Woods would miss the tournament cut by four strokes.

FIRST PGA WIN

At the age of 20 and in his fifth pro start, Tiger won the Las Vegas Invitational.

LAS VEGAS INVITATIONAL

PAY TO THE ORDER OF _____ _Tige_

Two Hundred Ninety

 BANK OF AMERICA

0014

October 6, 1996

Woods $ 297,000.00

n Thousand and 00/10

Tournament

Excerpted from Sports Illustrated, July 31, 2000

1996 Sportsman of the Year

Mere months into his PGA career, the questions turned
from how good Tiger Woods might be to whether
he could handle his coming superstardom

by GARY SMITH

It was ordinary. It was oh so ordinary. It was a salad, a dinner roll, a steak, a half potato, a slice of cake, a clinking fork, a podium joke, a ballroom full of white-linen-tablecloth conversation. Then a thick man with tufts of white hair rose from the head table. His voice trembled and his eyes teared and his throat gulped down sobs between words, and everything ordinary was cast out of the room.

He said, "Please forgive me . . . but sometimes I get very emotional . . . when I talk about my son. . . . My heart . . . fills with *so* . . . *much* . . . *joy* . . . when I realize . . . that this young man . . . is going to be able . . . to help so many people. . . . He will *transcend* this game . . . and bring to the world . . . a humanitarianism . . . which has never been known before. The world will be a better place to live in . . . by virtue of his existence . . . and his presence. . . . I acknowledge only a small part in that . . . in that I know that I was personally selected by God himself . . . to nurture this young man . . . and bring him to the point where he can make his contribution to humanity. . . . This is my treasure. . . . Please accept it . . . and use it wisely. . . . Thank you."

Blinking tears, the man found himself inside the arms of his son and the applause of the people, all up on their feet.

In the history of American celebrity, no father has ever spoken this way. Too many dads have deserted or died before their offspring reached this realm, but mostly they have fallen mute, the father's vision exceeded by the child's, leaving the child to wander, lost, through the sad and silly wilderness of modern fame.

So let us stand amidst this audience at last month's Fred Haskins Award dinner to honor America's outstanding college golfer of 1996, and take note as Tiger and Earl Woods embrace, for a new manner of celebrity is taking form before our eyes. Regard the 64-year-old African-American father, arm upon the superstar's shoulder, right where the chip is so often found, declaring that this boy will do more good for the world than any man who ever walked it. Gaze at the 20-year-old son, with the blood of four races in his veins, not flinching an inch from the yoke of his father's prophecy but already beginning to scent the complications. The son who stormed from behind to win a record third straight U.S. Amateur last August, turned pro and rang up scores in the 60s in 21 of his first 27 rounds, winning two PGA Tour events as he doubled and tripled the usual crowds and dramatically changed their look and age.

Now turn. Turn and look at us, the audience, standing in anticipation of something different, something pure. Quiet. Just below the applause, or within it, can you hear the grinding? That's the relentless chewing mechanism of fame, girding to grind the purity and the promise to dust. Not the promise of talent, but the bigger promise, the father's promise, the one that stakes everything on the boy's not becoming separated from his own humanity and from all the humanity crowding around him.

It's a fitting moment, while he's up there at the head table with the audience on its feet, to anoint Eldrick (Tiger) Woods—the rare athlete to establish himself immediately as the dominant figure in his sport—as SPORTS ILLUSTRATED's 1996 Sportsman of the Year. And to pose a question: Who will win? The machine . . . or the youth who has just entered its maw?

Tiger Woods will win. He'll fulfill his father's vision because of his mind, one that grows more still, more willful, more efficient, the greater the pressure upon him grows.

The machine will win because it has no mind. It flattens even as it lifts, trivializes even

as it exalts, spreads a man so wide and thin that he becomes margarine soon enough.

Tiger will win because of God's mind. *Can't you see the pattern?* Earl Woods asks. *Can't you see the signs?* "Tiger will do more than any other man in history to change the course of humanity," Earl says.

Sports history, Mr. Woods? Do you mean more than Joe Louis and Jackie Robinson, more than Muhammad Ali and Arthur Ashe? "More than any of them because he's more charismatic, more educated, more prepared for this than anyone."

Anyone, Mr. Woods? Your son will have more impact than Nelson Mandela, more than Gandhi, more than Buddha?

"Yes, because he has a larger forum than any of them. Because he's playing a sport that's international. Because he's qualified through his ethnicity to accomplish miracles. He's the bridge between the East and the West. There is no limit because he has the guidance. I don't know yet exactly what form this will take. But he is the Chosen One. He'll have the power to impact nations. Not people. Nations. The world is just getting a taste of his power."

Surely this is lunacy. Or are we just too myopic to see? One thing is certain: We are witnessing the first volley of an epic encounter, the machine at its mightiest confronting the individual groomed all his life to conquer it and turn it to his use. The youth who has been exposed to its power since he toddled onto *The Mike Douglas Show* at three, the set of *That's Incredible!* at five, the boy who has been steeled against the silky seduction to which so many before him have succumbed. The one who, by all appearances, brings more psychological balance, more sense of self, more consciousness of possibility to the battlefield than any of his predecessors.

This is in the air the boy breathes for 20 years, and it becomes bone fact for him, marrow knowledge. When asked about it, he merely nods in acknowledgment of it, *assents* to it; *of course* he believes it's true. So failure, in the rare visits it pays him, is not failure. It's just life pausing to teach him a lesson he needs in order to go where he's inevitably going. And success, no matter how much sooner than expected it comes to the door, always finds him dressed and ready to welcome it. "Did you *ever* see yourself doing this so soon?" a commentator breathlessly asks him seconds after his first pro victory, on Oct. 6 in Las Vegas, trying to elicit wonder and awe on live TV. "Yeah," Tiger responds. "I kind of did." And sleep comes to him so easily: In the midst of conversation, in a car, in a plane, off he goes, into the slumber of the destined. "I don't see any of this as scary or a burden," Tiger says. "I see it as fortunate. I've always known where I wanted to go in life. I've never let anything deter me. This is my purpose. *It will unfold.*"

No sports star in the history of American celebrity has spoken this way. Maybe, somehow, Tiger *can* win.

The machine will win. It must win because it too is destiny, five billion destinies leaning against one. There are ways to keep the hordes back, a media expert at Nike tells Tiger. Make broad gestures when you speak. Keep a club in your hands and take practice swings, or stand with one foot well out in front of the other, in almost a karate stance. That will give you room to breathe. Two weeks later, surrounded by a pen-wielding mob in La Quinta, Calif., in late November, just before the Skins Game, the instruction fails. Tiger survives, but his shirt and slacks are ruined, felt-tip-dotted to death.

The machine will win because it will wear the young man down, cloud his judgment, steal his sweetness, the way it does just before the Buick Challenge in Pine Mountain, Ga., at the end of September. It will make his eyes drop when the fans' gaze reaches for his, his voice growl at their clawing hands, his body sag onto a sofa after a practice round and then rise and walk across the room and suddenly stop in bewilderment. "I couldn't even remember what I'd just gotten off the couch for, two seconds before," he says. "I was like mashed potatoes. Total mush."

So he walks. Pulls out on the eve of the Buick Challenge, pulls out of the Fred Haskins Award dinner to honor him, and goes home. See, maybe Tiger can win. He can just turn his back on the machine and walk. Awards? Awards to Tiger are like echoes, voices bouncing off the walls, repeating what a truly confident man has already heard inside his own head. The Jack Nicklaus Award, the one Jack himself was supposed to present to Tiger live on ABC during the Memorial tournament last spring? Tiger would have blown it off if Wally Goodwin, his coach at Stanford during the two years he played there before turning pro, hadn't insisted that he show up.

The instant Tiger walks away from the Buick Challenge and the Haskins dinner, the hounds start yapping. See, that's why the machine will win. It's got all those damn heel-nippers. Little mutts on the PGA Tour resenting how swiftly the 20-year-old was ordained, how hastily he was invited to play practice rounds with Nicklaus and Arnold Palmer, with Greg Norman and Ray Floyd and Nick Faldo and Fred Couples. And big dogs snapping too. Tom Kite quoted as saying, "I can't ever remember being tired when I was 20," and Peter Jacobsen quoted, "You can't compare Tiger to Nicklaus and Palmer anymore because they never [walked out]."

He rests for a week, stunned by the criticism— "I thought those people were my friends," he says. He never second-guesses his decision to turn pro, but he sees what he surrendered. "I miss college," he says. "I miss hanging out with my friends, getting in a

> **"I don't see any of this as scary or a burden," Tiger says. "I see it as fortunate. I've always known where I wanted to go in life. I've never let anything deter me. This is my purpose. It will unfold."**

little trouble. I have to be so guarded now. I miss sitting around drinking beer and talking half the night. There's no one my own age to hang out with anymore because almost everyone my age is in college. I'm a target for everybody now, and there's nothing I can do about it. My mother was right when she said that turning pro would take away my youth. But golfwise, there was nothing left for me in college."

He reemerges after the week's rest and rushes from four shots off the lead on the final day to win the Las Vegas Invitational in sudden death. The world's waiting for him again, this time with reinforcements. Letterman and Leno want him as a guest; *GQ* calls about a cover; *Cosby*, along with almost every other sitcom you can think of, offers to write an episode revolving around Tiger, if only he'll appear. Kids dress up as Tiger for Halloween—did anyone ever dress up as Arnie or Jack?—and Michael Jordan declares that his only hero on earth is Tiger Woods. Pepsi is dying to have him cut a commercial for one of its soft drinks aimed at Generation Xers; Nike and Titleist call in chits

for the $40 million and $20 million contracts he signed; money managers are eager to know how he wants his millions invested; women walk onto the course during a practice round and ask for his hand in marriage; kids stampede over and under ropes and chase him from the 18th hole to the clubhouse; piles of phone messages await him when he returns to his hotel room. "Why," Tiger asks, "do so many people want a piece of me?"

Because something deeper than conventional stardom is at work here, something so spontaneous and subconscious that words have trouble going there. It's a communal craving, a public aching for a superstar free of anger and arrogance and obsession with self. It's a hollow place that chimes each time Tiger and his parents strike the theme of father and mother and child love, each time Tiger stands at a press conference and declares, "They have raised me well, and I truly believe they have taught me to accept full responsibility for all aspects of my life." During the making of a Titleist commercial in November, a makeup woman is so moved listening to Earl describe his bond with Tiger that she

decides to contact her long-estranged father. "See what I mean?" cries Earl. "Did *you* affect someone that way today? Did anyone else there? It's destiny, man. It's something bigger than me."

Let's be honest. The machine will win because you can't work both sides of this street. The machine will win because you can't transcend wearing 16 Nike swooshes, you can't move human hearts while you're busy pushing sneakers. Gandhi didn't hawk golf balls, did he? Jackie Robinson was spared that fate because he came and went while Madison Avenue was still teething. Ali became a symbol instead of a logo because of boxing's disrepute and because of the attrition of cells in the basal ganglia of his brain. Who or what will save Tiger Woods?

Did someone say *Buddha*?

Every year near his birthday, Tiger goes with his mother to a Buddhist temple and makes a gift of rice, sugar and salt to the monks there who have renounced all material goods. A mother-of-pearl Buddha given to Tiger by his Thai grandfather watches over him while he sleeps, and a gold Buddha hangs from the chain on his neck. "I like Buddhism because it's a whole way of being and living," Tiger says. "It's based on discipline and respect and personal responsibility. I like Asian culture better than ours because of that.

"I believe in Buddhism. Not every aspect, but most of it. So I take bits and pieces. I don't believe that human beings can achieve ultimate enlightenment, because humans have flaws. I don't want to get rid of all my wants and desires. I can enjoy material things, but that doesn't mean I need them. It doesn't matter to me whether I live in a place like this"—the golf club in his hand makes a sweep of the Orlando villa—"or in a shack. I'd be fine in a shack, as long as I could play some golf. I'll do the commercials for Nike and for Titleist, but there won't be much

more than that. I have no desire to be the king of endorsement money."

On the morning after he decides to turn pro, there's a knock on his hotel room door. It's Tiger's agent, Hughes Norton, bleary-eyed but exhilarated after a late-night round of negotiations with Nike. He explains to Tiger and Earl that the benchmark for contract endorsements in golf is Norman's reported $2.5 million-a-year deal with Reebok. Then, gulping down hard on the *yabba-dabba-doo* rising up his throat, Norton announces Nike's offer: $40 million for five years, *eight mil a year*. "Over *three* times what Norman gets!" Norton exults.

Silence.

"Guys, do you realize this is more than Nike pays any athlete in salary, even *Jordan*?"

Silence.

"Finally," Norton says now, recalling that morning, "Tiger says, '*Mmmm-hmmm*,' and I say, 'That's *it*? Mmmm-hmmm?' No 'Omigod.' No slapping five or 'Ya-hooo!' So I say, 'Let me go through this again, guys.' Finally Tiger says, 'Guess that's pretty amazing.' That's *it*. When I made the deal with Titleist a day later, I went back to them saying, 'I'm almost embarrassed to tell you this one. Titleist is offering a little more than $20 million over five years.'"

On the Monday morning after his first pro tournament, a week after the two megadeals, Tiger scans the tiny print on the sports page under Milwaukee Open money earnings and finds his name. *Tiger Woods: $2,544.* "That's my money," he exclaims. "I earned this!"

See, maybe Tiger *can* win.

How? How can he win when there are so many insects under so many rocks? Several more death threats arrive just before the Skins Game, prompting an increase in his plainclothes security force, which is already larger than anyone knows. His agent's first instinct is to trash every piece of hate mail delivered to

IMG, but Tiger won't permit it. Every piece of racist filth must be saved and given to him. At Stanford he kept one letter taped to his wall. Fuel comes in the oddest forms.

The audience, in its hunger for goodness, swallows hard over the Nike ad that heralds Tiger's entrance into the professional ranks. The words that flash on the screen over images of Tiger—*There are still courses in the United States I am not allowed to play because of the color of my skin. I've heard I'm not ready for you. Are you ready for me?*—ooze the very attitude from which many in the audience are seeking relief. The media backlash is swift: The Tiger Woods who used to tell the press, "The only time I think about race is when the media ask me"—whoa, what happened to *him*?

What happened to him was a steady accretion of experiences, also known as a life. What happened, just weeks before he was born, was a fusillade of limes and BBs rattling the Woods house in Cypress, Calif., one of the limes shattering the kitchen window, splashing glass all around the pregnant Tida,

to welcome the middle-class subdivision's first non-Caucasian family.

What happened was a gang of older kids seizing Tiger on his first day of kindergarten, tying him to a tree, hurling rocks at him, calling him monkey and nigger. And Tiger, at age five, telling no one what happened for several days, trying to absorb what this meant about himself and his world.

What happened was the Look, as Tiger and Earl came to call it, the uneasy, silent stare they received in countless country-club locker rooms and restaurants. "Something a white person could never understand," says Tiger, "unless he went to Africa and suddenly found himself in the middle of a tribe." What happened was Tiger's feeling pressured to leave a driving range just two years ago, not far from his family's California home, because a resident watching Tiger's drives rocket into the nearby protective netting reported that a Black teenager was trying to bombard his house.

What happened was the cold shoulder Earl got when he took his tyke to play at the Navy

"I miss college," Tiger says. "I miss hanging out with my friends, getting in a little trouble. I have to be so guarded now. I miss sitting around drinking beer and talking half the night....My mother was right when she said that turning pro would take away my youth. But golfwise, there was nothing left for me in college."

Golf Course in Cypress—"a club," Earl says, "composed mostly of retired naval personnel who knew Blacks only as cooks and servers, and along comes me, a retired lieutenant colonel outranking 99 percent of them, and I have the nerve to take up golf at 42 and immediately become a low handicap and beat them, and then I have the *audacity* to have this kid. Well, they had to do something. They took away Tiger's playing privileges twice, said he was too young, even though there were other kids too young who they let play. The second time it happened, I went up to the pro who had done it and made a bet. I said, 'If you'll spot my three-year-old just one stroke a hole, nine holes, playing off the same tees, and he beats you, will you certify him?' The pro started laughing and said, 'Sure.' Tiger beat him by two strokes, got certified, then the members went over the pro's head and kicked him out again. That's when we switched him to another course."

Beat them. That was his parents' solution for each banishment, each Look. Hold your tongue, hew to every rule and *beat them.* Tiger Woods is the son of the first Black baseball player in the Big Seven, a catcher back in the early '50s, before the conference became the Big Eight. A man who had to leave his Kansas State teammates on road trips and travel miles to stay in motels for Blacks; who had to go to the back door of restaurant kitchens to be fed while his teammates dined inside; who says, "This is the most racist society in the world—I *know* that." A man who learned neither to extinguish his anger nor spray it but to quietly convert it into animus, the determination to enter the system and overcome it by turning its own tools against it. A Green Berets explosives expert whose mind naturally ran that way, whose response, upon hearing Tiger rave about the security in his new walled community, was, "*I* could get in. I could blow up the clubhouse and be

gone before they ever knew what hit them." A father who saw his son, from the beginning, as the one who would enter one of America's last Caucasian bastions, the PGA Tour, and overthrow it from within in a manner that would make it smile and ask for more. "Been planning that one for 20 years," says Earl. "See, you don't turn it into hatred. You turn it into something positive. So many athletes who reach the top now had things happen to them as children that created hostility, and they bring that hostility with them. But that hostility uses up energy. If you can do it without the chip on the shoulder, it frees up all that energy to create."

It's not until Stanford, where Tiger takes an African-American history course and stays up half the night in dormitories talking with people of every shade of skin, that his experiences begin to crystallize. "What I realized is that even though I'm mathematically Asian—if anything—if you have one drop of Black blood in the United States, you're Black," says Tiger. "And how important it is for this country to talk about this subject. It's not me to blow my horn, the way I come across in that Nike ad, or to say things quite that way. But I felt it was worth it because the message needed to be said. You can't say something like that in a polite way. Golf has shied away from this for too long. Some clubs have brought in tokens, but nothing has really changed. I hope what I'm doing can change that."

But don't overestimate race's proportion in the fuel that propels Tiger Woods. Don't look for traces of race in the astonishing rubble at his feet on the Sunday after he lost the Texas Open by two strokes and returned to his hotel room and snapped a putter in two with one violent lift of his knee. Then another putter. And another. And another and another—eight in all before his rage was spent and he was ready to begin considering the loss's philosophical lesson. "That volcano of competitive fire, that comes from me," says Earl. A volcano that's mostly an elite athlete's need to win, a need far more immediate than that of changing the world.

No, don't overestimate race, but don't overlook it, either. When Tiger is asked about racism, about the effect it has on him when he senses it in the air, he has a golf club in his hands. He takes the club by the neck, his eyes flashing hot and cold at once, and gives it a short upward thrust. He says, "It makes me want to stick it right up their asses." Pause. "On the golf course."

The machine will win because there is so much of the old man's breath in the boy . . . and how long can the old man keep breathing? At 2 a.m., hours before the second round of the Tour Championship in Tulsa on Oct. 25, the phone rings in Tiger's hotel room. It's Mom. Pop's in an ambulance, on his way to a Tulsa hospital. He's just had his second heart attack.

The Tour Championship? The future of humanity? The hell with 'em. Tiger's at the old man's bedside in no time, awake most of the night. Tiger's out of contention in the Tour Championship by dinnertime, with a second-round 78, his worst till then as a pro. "There are things more important than golf," he says.

The old man survives—and sees the pattern at work, of course. He's got to throw away the cigarettes. He's got to quit ordering the cholesterol special for breakfast. "I've got to shape up now, God's telling me," Earl says, "or I won't be around for the last push, the last lesson." The one about how to ride the tsunami of runaway fame.

The machine will win because no matter how complicated it all seems now, it is simpler than it will ever be. The boy will marry one day, and the happiness of two people will lie in his hands. Children will follow, and it will become his job to protect three or four or five people from the molars of the machine. Imagine the din of the grinding in five, 10, 15 years, when the boy reaches his golfing prime.

The machine will win because the whole notion is so ludicrous to begin with, a kid clutching an eight-iron changing the course of humanity. No, of course not, there won't be thousands of people sitting in front of tanks because of Tiger Woods. He won't bring about the overthrow of a tyranny or spawn a religion that one day will number 300 million devotees.

But maybe Pop is onto something without quite seeing what it is. Maybe it has to do with timing: The appearance of his son when America is turning the corner to a century in which the country's faces of color will nearly equal those that are white. Maybe, every now and then, a man gets swallowed by the machine, but the machine is changed more than he is.

For when we swallow Tiger Woods, the yellow-black-red-white man, we swallow something much more significant than Jordan or Charles Barkley. We swallow hope in the American experiment, in the pell-mell jumbling of genes. We swallow the belief that the face of the future is not necessarily a bitter or bewildered face; that it might even, one day, be something like Tiger Woods's face: handsome and smiling and ready to kick all comers' asses.

We see a woman, 50-ish and Caucasian, well-coiffed and tailored—the woman we see at every country club—walk up to Tiger Woods before he receives the Haskins Award and say, "When I watch you taking on all those other players, Tiger, I feel like I'm watching my own son" . . . and we feel the quivering of the cosmic compass that occurs when human beings look into the eyes of someone of another color and see their own flesh and blood. ●

TIGER TAKES OFF

Chapter 2

1997 MASTERS

Tiger hit his final putt at 18, as the scoreboard told the story of his dominance.

1997 MASTERS

Tiger, with guidance from caddie Fluff Cowan, shot a second-round 66 to take a lead he would not relinquish.

TIGER WOODS

1997 MASTERS

Tiger and Earl celebrated with
a hug by the 18th green with
Kultida (right) alongside.

Excerpted from SPORTS ILLUSTRATED, April 21, 2000

The 1997 Masters

With a runaway win in his first major as a
professional, Tiger made it clear that the hype was
real and that golf would never be the same

by RICK REILLY

Short and pudgy, he pushed through the crowd, elbowing and worming his way, not stopping for any of the cries of "Heyyy, watchit!" as he went. At last he popped through to the front and craned his neck down the line, wide-eyed, hoping to see what he had come for. As Tiger Woods strode past, Jack Nicholson slapped him on the back and grinned, same as everybody else.

It didn't matter who you were; if you were there the week everything changed in golf, you just had to reach out and touch a piece of history. Almost 50 years to the day after Jackie Robinson broke major league baseball's color barrier, at Augusta National, a club that no Black man was allowed to join until six years ago, at the tournament whose founder, Clifford Roberts, once said, "As long as I'm alive, golfers will be white, and caddies will be Black," a 21-year-old Black man delivered the greatest performance ever seen in a golf major.

Someday Eldrick (Tiger) Woods, a mixed-race kid with a middle-class background who grew up on a municipal course in the sprawl of Los Angeles, may be hailed as the greatest golf-er who ever lived, but it is likely that his finest day will always be the overcast Sunday in Augusta when he humiliated the world's best golfers, shot 18-under-par 70-66-65-69—270 (the lowest score in tournament history) and won the Masters by a preposterous 12 shots. It was the soundest whipping in a major this century and second only to Old Tom Morris's 13-shot triumph in the 1862 British Open.

When Tiger finally slipped into his green champion's jacket, his 64-year-old father, Earl, drank in a long look and said, "Green and Black go well together, don't they?"

So golf is trying to get used to the fact that the man who will rule the game for the next 20 years shaves twice a week and has been drinking legally for almost three months now. "He's more dominant over the guys he's playing against than I ever was over the ones I played against," marveled no less an authority than Jack Nicklaus, whose 17-under Masters record of 271 had held up for 32 years. "He's so long, he reduces the course to nothing. Absolutely nothing."

It was something to see the way a 6'2", 155-pounder with a 30-inch waist crumbled one of golf's masterpieces into bite-sized pieces. The longest club he hit into a par-4 all week was a seven-iron. On each of the first two days he hit a wedge into the 500-yard par-5 15th hole—for his *second* shot. Honey, he shrunk the course. On Saturday his seven birdies were set up by his nine-iron, pitching wedge, sand wedge, putter, nine-iron, putter and sand wedge. Meanwhile, the rest of the field was trying to catch him with five-irons and three-woods and rosary beads. When Nicklaus said last year that Woods would win 10 green jackets, everybody figured he was way off. We just never thought his number was low.

Woods's performance was the most outstanding in Augusta National history, and that figured, because he stood out all week. He stood out because of the color of his skin against the mostly white crowds. He stood out because of his youth in a field that averaged 38 years. He stood out because of the flabbergasting length of his drives —323 yards on average, 25 yards longer than the next player on the chart. He stood out for the steeliness in his eyes and for the unshakable purpose in his step. "He may be 21," said Mike (Fluff) Cowan, his woolly caddie, "but he ain't no 21 inside those ropes."

It was a week like nobody had ever seen at Augusta National. Never before had scalpers' prices for a weekly badge been so high. Some were asking $10,000. Even after it was all done, a seemingly useless badge was fetching up to $50 outside the club's gates. Never

before had one player attracted such a large following. Folks might have come out with the intention of watching another golfer, but each day the course seemed to tilt toward wherever Woods was playing. Everybody else was Omar Uresti. Never before had so many people stayed at the course so long, filling the stands behind the practice range, 1,500 strong, to watch a lone player hit thrilling wedge shots under the darkening Georgia sky. It was the highest-rated golf telecast in history, yet guys all over the country had to tell their wives that the reason they couldn't help plant the rhododendrons was that they needed to find out whether the champion would win by 11 or 12.

Away from the golf course, Woods didn't look much like a god. He ate burgers and fries, played Ping-Pong and P-I-G with his buddies, screamed at video games and drove his parents to the far end of their rented house. Michael Jordan called, and Nike czar Phil Knight came by, and the FedExes and telegrams from across the world piled up on the coffee table, but none of it seemed to matter much. What did matter was the Mortal Kombat video game and the fact that he was Motaro and his Stanford buddy Jerry Chang was Kintaro and he had just ripped Kintaro's mutant head off and now there was green slime spewing out and Tiger could roar in his best creature voice, "Mmmmmwaaaaannnnnggh!"

What's weird is that this was the only Masters in history that began on the back nine on Thursday and ended on Saturday night. For the first nine holes of the tournament the three-time reigning U.S. Amateur champion looked very amateurish. He kept flinching with his driver, visiting many of Augusta's manicured forests, bogeying 1, 4, 8 and 9 and generally being much more about Woods than about Tigers. His 40 was by two shots the worst starting nine ever for a Masters winner.

But something happened to him as he walked to the 10th tee, something that separates him from other humans. He fixed his swing, right there, in his mind. He is nothing if not a quick study. In the six Augusta rounds he played as an amateur, he never broke par, mostly because he flew more greens than Delta with his irons and charged for birdie with his putter, often making bogey instead. This year, though, he realized he had to keep his approach shots below the hole and keep the leash on his putter. "We learned how to hit feeders," Cowan said. Woods figured out how to relax and appreciate the six-inch tap-in. (For the week he had zero three-putts.) And now, at the turn on Thursday, he realized he was bringing the club almost parallel to the ground on his backswing—"way too long for me"—so he shortened his swing right then and there.

He immediately grooved a two-iron down the 10th fairway and birdied the hole from 18 feet. Then he birdied the par-3 12th with a deft chip-in from behind the green and the 13th with two putts. He eagled the 15th with a wedge to four feet. When he finished birdie-par, he had himself a back-nine 30 for a two-under 70—your basic CPR nine. Woods was only three shots behind the first-day leader, John Huston, who moved in front at 18 by holing a five-iron from 180 yards for eagle and then dropped from sight the next day with a double-par beagle 10 on the 13th. Playing in the twosome ahead of Huston, Woods had eagled the same hole after hitting an eight-iron to 20 feet, vaulting into the outright lead, one he would never relinquish.

By Friday night you could feel the sea change coming. Woods's 66 was the finest round of the day, and his lead was three over Colin Montgomerie.

Saturday was nearly mystical. As the rest of the field slumped, Woods just kept ringing up birdies. He tripled his lead from three to nine with a bogeyless 65.

That night there was this loopiness, this giddy sense, even among the players, of needing to laugh in the face of something you never thought you'd see. A 21-year-old in his first major as a pro was about to obliterate every record, and it was almost too big a thought to be thunk. "I might have a chance," said Paul Stankowski, who trailed by 10, "if I make five or six birdies in the first two or three holes."

Only 47-year-old Tom Kite, who would finish second in the same sense that Germany finished second in World War II, refused to give up. He was a schnauzer with his teeth locked on the tailpipe of a Greyhound bus as it was pulling into beltway traffic. How can you be so optimistic when Woods is leading by nine shots? "Well," said Kite, "we've got it down to single digits, don't we?"

The last round was basically a coronation parade with occasional stops to hit a dimpled object. Woods went out on the front nine in even par, then birdied the 11th, the 13th and the 14th and parred the 16th with a curvaceous two-putt. "After that, I knew I could bogey in and win," he said. That's a bit of an understatement, of course. He could've quintuple-bogeyed in and won. He could've used nothing but his putter, his umbrella and a rolled-up *Mad* magazine and won.

He wanted the record, though, and for that there was one last challenge—the 18th. On his tee shot a photographer clicked twice on the backswing, and Woods lurched, hooking his drive way left. On this hole, though, the only trouble comes if you're short or right, and Woods has not been short since grade school. He had a wedge shot to the green—if only he could get his wedge. Fluff was lost. "Fluff!" Woods hollered, jumping as if on a pogo stick to see over the gallery. Fluff finally found him as the crowd chanted, "Fluff! Fluff!" It was not exactly tense.

Still, Woods needed a five-footer for par, and when he sank it, he threw his trademark uppercut. The tournament he had talked about winning since he was five, the tournament he had watched on tape almost every night in his little suburban bedroom all those years, the tournament he had wanted more than all the others, was his, and the dream had only just begun. He was now the youngest man by two years to win the Masters and the first Black man to win any major.

So golf is all new now. Everything is a fight for *place*. *Win* seems to be spoken for. If you are the tournament director of a PGA Tour event, you better do whatever's necessary to get Tiger Woods, because your Wendy's-Shearson Lehman Pensacola Classic is the junior varsity game without him.

Of course, much more than golf was changed at Augusta National last week. As Woods made his way from Butler Cabin and an interview with CBS, he brought his phalanx of Pinkerton guards and other escorts to a sudden stop. Out of the corner of his eye Woods spied Lee Elder, the man who at 39 had finally won a PGA Tour event, the Monsanto Open, earning his invitation as the first Black man to play the Masters, in 1975, the year Tiger was born. Woods knew Elder's story, knew about Teddy Rhodes, too, the star of the Black golf circuit in the 1940s, who might've won here if he'd had the chance;

and of Charlie Sifford, who outplayed Masters champions like Doug Ford and Gay Brewer regularly on the Tour but never qualified to play here; and of his own father, who was the first Black man to play baseball in the Big Eight and was often forced to stay in separate hotels and eat in separate restaurants, apart from his teammates. Tiger knows all the stories he never had to live, so he stopped and put a giant bear hug on Elder. "Thanks for making this possible," Woods whispered in his ear, and then the parade swept on. Elder had tears in his eyes.

At the very end Woods made it into the elegant Augusta National clubhouse dining room for the traditional winner's dinner. As he entered, the members and their spouses stood and applauded politely, as they have for each champion, applauded as he made his way to his seat at the head table under a somber oil painting of President Eisenhower. But clear in the back, near a service entrance, the Black cooks and waiters and busboys ripped off their oven mitts and plastic gloves, put their dishes and trays down for a while, hung their napkins over their arms and clapped the loudest and the hardest and the longest for the kind of winner they never dreamed would come through those doors. ●

"

When Tiger finally slipped into his green champion's jacket, his 64-year-old father, Earl, drank in a long look and said, "Green and Black go well together, don't they?"

Tiger delivered his iconic combination of big shot and fist pump when he holed in a chip at the 14th hole, on his way to a two-shot victory.

1999 MEMORIAL

1999 PGA CHAMPIONSHIP

Tiger captured his second major and 11th Tour win at the Medinah Country Club.

1999 PGA

As playing partner Mike Weir
(above) faded on Sunday,
Tiger held off Sergio García by
one stroke to claim the trophy.

Team USA celebrated a wild comeback win at the 1999 Ryder Cup in Brookline, Mass.; Tiger did his part on Sunday by defeating Team Europe's Andrew Coltart 3 and 2.

1999 RYDER CUP

Excerpted from SPORTS ILLUSTRATED, April 3, 2000

Coming of Age

With two majors and 18 Tour wins to his credit,
Tiger's superstardom was in full flower, and he was
transitioning from boy wonder to man in command

by S.L. PRICE

The last time it happened, his son stood over the ball on a blistering Sunday at Medinah (Ill.) Country Club. Sergio García, young and eager, threatened disaster from just one stroke back. Tiger Woods held the lead at the 1999 PGA Championship, but his putter had let him down again and again. For once he looked vulnerable. Eight feet from the cup on 17 now. Holing the par putt would erase the pressure, would virtually clinch the victory. His second major. His reputation intact.

Tiger stood over the ball. He heard the voice of his father, Earl, high and hollow, sounding in his head. He didn't know where it was coming from. Memory? Fear? Earl insists that he can do this anytime, talk to his son when he's on the other side of the course, talk to him through a television set all the way at the other end of the earth. Earl did it that day from his hotel room in Chicago, softly speaking to his son's image as it glowed on the screen: *Tiger. This is a must-make putt. Trust your stroke. Trust your stroke.*

Tiger heard, trusted, sent the ball rolling. It dropped into history. That night at the victory party, Tiger smiled at Earl and said, "I heard you, Pop."

The first time it happened, Tiger was 12. San Diego, junior world championships, final hole: He hit an approach shot over the green, needed to get up and down for the win. Earl, standing behind the green where Tiger couldn't see him, began muttering to himself, *Don't do anything stupid. Put the ball on the green and trust your putting.* Tiger pitched, putted, won. He came sprinting over the grass, yelling, "I heard you, Daddy! I heard you!"

"That's when we knew," Earl says. "He knows where I am at all times."

———————————

Everything bends to him now. Parents, opponents, friends, interviewers, tour flacks, sponsors, tour directors, TV networks—all wait for Tiger to make the call. All hope he will give a minute, pay them just a little more attention, but they understand if he can't, and they wait some more. Greatness gives you power, and power allows you to control your world, and if your world keeps expanding beyond the wealthy little fiefdom of professional golf and into the mad plastic nation of pure celebrity, so be it. Woods is 24 years old and the biggest, richest, most powerful athlete in his game. He doesn't worry about money. He doesn't worry about what people think. His greatness has set him free.

Last fall, during a Ryder Cup practice round, Woods and Tom Lehman were playing alternate shots—one teed off on the odd holes, the other on the even—and Woods stood waiting for Lehman to tee up on the sixth. A fan with a thick Boston accent rasped, "Come on, Tigah! Hit one!" Woods stared into space. "Hit a ball, Tigah! Come on!" Woods waited for Lehman to drive and then strolled away. "Hit one for me, Tigah!" Woods didn't turn, wave, shrug. Nothing. Finally, here it came: "Tigah! You suck!"

"You get that a lot?" Lehman asked.

"Every day," Woods said.

"Most guys, it'd bother them or piss them off, but with Tiger it's just water off a duck's back," Lehman says. "It didn't even faze him."

Almost nothing does. Even the stresses of sport, the pressure that made Roger Maris's hair fall out in clumps, hold little power over Woods. He doesn't crack. He doesn't blow leads. When, last fall and winter, he captivated the country by winning six straight PGA Tour events, churning up talk about his breaking Byron Nelson's unbreakable record of 11 consecutive tournament victories, Woods showed no sign of noticing, much less wilting under, the mushrooming mania. That's because he found what everyone else considered astounding to be bogus. He'd lost a non-Tour event during the streak, so while his peers marveled and the scribes oohed and aahed, Woods had no use for any of it. "That wasn't a streak," he says. "I look at a streak as *I don't lose*—literally."

Such exactitude can be deflating to his admirers, but Woods's ambition leaves him no choice. He has won 18 Tour events in his 3½ years as a pro, gathered $45 million in endorsements and already set the record for career winnings with $14.5 million, but to him those are mere numbers. He sets for himself a higher standard—he wants to be, simply, the greatest golfer of all time—and he rightly regards himself as not only the one proper custodian of his game but also its only bona fide judge. Woods doesn't care what a fan or some bloated golf writer or the average former pro with a microphone says. He doesn't need what they have to give.

This is cold, but who's going to argue? Woods broke the tournament records for 72-hole score (270) and margin of victory (12 strokes) at the Masters in 1997 and won that PGA at Medinah for his other major, staying roughly even with his Moby-Dick, Jack Nicklaus, at the same point in their careers. Woods's unique stature has forced a revolution that now washes over every corner of the pro game: Everyone in golf has been obliged to adjust to the fact that because Tiger rules, there are plenty of Tiger Rules. Tournament security has been beefed up. Tiger never commits to an event until the last minute. But few complain: Ratings skyrocket whenever he plays; purses have just about doubled in the last four years largely because of his soaring popularity; Nike's golf division has grown from $100 million to $250 million since Tiger signed a contract with the company four years ago. "We all ought to be thankful he's out here," says Tour veteran Steve Pate. "Because of him we're playing for a helluva lot more money."

Fat times always make it easier for subjects to bow their heads, but having his ring kissed has interested Woods far less than exercising suzerainty over his court. After several missteps following his leap onto the Tour in 1996, he has seized control of the career once steered by his father—the chain of command now begins and ends with Tiger—and purged everyone from the original Team Tiger except swing coach Butch Harmon. One by one they found themselves outside looking in: Sports psychologist Jay Brunza (who retains a position on the board of the Tiger Woods Foundation), lawyer John Merchant, agent Hughes Norton and, last year, celebrated caddie Mike (Fluff) Cowan. In all cases, Woods father and son say, Tiger

made the decision to cut the associate loose (though Merchant says he was fired by Earl). "I haven't talked to Tiger since," says Merchant of his dismissal in December 1996, after several years as an adviser to Earl and five months as Tiger's lawyer. "I was puzzled by it. But lawyers come and go, so I got out of Dodge."

The firings came for different and, perhaps, understandable reasons. Brunza, a Navy captain who caddied for Tiger when Tiger was in the juniors, carried his bag less once Tiger went off to Stanford. As for Cowan, caddies have about as much job security as migrant workers. Many observers note, however, that Cowan, Merchant and Norton all shared the fatal flaws of being older than Tiger and having outsized personalities that didn't jibe with his reserved style. The dismissals had a chilling finality. "Very tough, unemotional, very cold," says one longtime Tiger watcher. "With all his money and achievement, it won't matter, but there's this total lack of loyalty to anybody. Brunza, Merchant, Norton, Cowan—dumped. And Butch Harmon... someday. Tiger coldly cuts through and moves on."

> **After several missteps following his leap onto the Tour in 1996, he has seized control of the career once steered by his father—the chain of command now begins and ends with Tiger—and purged everyone from the original Team Tiger except swing coach Butch Harmon.**

Woods explains the firings vaguely: "You just want a better fit, just want things a little bit better." But if his off-course ruthlessness is merely a way to keep things simple, it dovetails with his on-course reputation for hammering opponents into the turf—"stepping on the neck," as the Woods family so delicately puts it. Yet Woods has also learned how to handle his dominance with grace. After Rocco Mediate fended off Woods and Justin Leonard in the final round to win the 1999 Phoenix Open (Mediate's first win in six years, including an absence from the Tour for the better part of two years for major back surgery), he was stunned when Woods approached him and whispered, "Glad to have you back."

In February, on the day her son gutted Michael Campbell 5 and 4 in the opening round of the Andersen Consulting Match Play Championship at La Costa in Carlsbad, Calif., leaving a carcass where the winter's second-hottest golfer once stood, Kultida Woods sat on a couch outside the locker room. Suddenly a player stuck a hand in front of her. "My name is Olin Browne," he said. "I played with Tiger at the Sprint International last year, just after he won the PGA, and I wanted to tell you that you raised a good man. He's a *good* man." Browne walked off. Tida beamed.

"This is what a mother loves to hear," she said. Tida went on to tell how she was the law in the house when Tiger was growing up in the Los Angeles suburb of Cypress; how she told him, "You will never, never ruin my reputation as a parent, because I will beat you"; how she—not her Vietnam-veteran husband—was the one who instilled in Tiger a cutthroat approach to the game. "I said, 'Go after them, kill them,'" Tida said, her English weighted by a heavy Thai accent. "'When you're finished, now it's sportsmanship. Before that, go for that throat. Don't let your opponent up.'"

Told that Earl says he would like Tiger to develop a more tender side as his career moves along, Tida laughed. "That's Dad," she said. "Dad wants him to be more compassionate. He's Green Beret and all, but he's more compassionate than I am. Tiger's personality is more like mine than Dad's." Asked if that also applies off the course, Tida nodded. "When Tiger says no, don't ever go ask him again—that's it," she said. "When he moves along, out, he won't come back. He's more like Mom: When I say 'Enough,' don't ever come ask me again. I cut and move on. Tiger's more like me."

Tiger's father is courting death now. There's no prognosis, but Earl, 68, has had three open-heart surgeries, and he won't stop with the bad food and the Merits. His energy drains away so easily that he tends to doze off. He's short of breath. His refusal to change old habits hits his family like a suicide note. "He said, 'This is the way I want to live my life,'" Tida, 55, says. "But I want to see my son's future. I want to see my grandkids. Dad wants to check out first? Fine with me. But I want to stay longer."

What does their son think? Tiger, says Earl, is "reconciled" to his father's condition and stubbornness, and he's mostly gone anyway. Earl and Tida maintain a close, admiring relationship, but Earl lives in the old family house in Cypress, Calif., while Tida lives a few miles down Interstate 5 in a home Tiger bought for her in Tustin. She drives to Cypress often, sometimes just to clean house. Earl goes to tournaments but never walks the course; he sees his son win on TV. That, mostly, is where he talks to Tiger.

"We don't have to communicate with each other to validate our relationship," Earl said at La Costa. "I don't have to say 'Oh, Tiger, I love you.' Are you kidding me? I haven't talked to Tiger in two weeks, and he was in Los Angeles

TIGER WOODS

and San Diego. No big deal. All this rumor crap that came up about him being engaged? I didn't have to talk to Tiger. I know him. I trust him to come talk to me before making a decision like that. I laughed when I heard the damn thing."

Earl is the most conspicuous deletion from Team Tiger, though no one discusses it much. He's still chairman of the Tiger Woods Foundation and president of the Tiger Woods Corporation, which owns Tiger's on- and off-course rights, but mostly his son works alone. This was the plan. "I raised Tiger to leave me," Earl says, and that's exactly what happened.

"When I first turned pro, he was always there for me, we could talk at night," Tiger says. "Then as I began to understand what it took to play out here and the obligations that come with being a professional golfer, he gradually did what most parents do: Let their child go. He's always there for guidance when asked. He may observe from the outside and may offer a suggestion every now and then. But he has never said, 'You really need to do this.' Now I do whatever I want to do."

Tiger has a condominium in Manhattan Beach, Calif.—"his bachelor house," Tida calls it—and it's a place she doesn't dare visit. "Do you want Mom to be around to see the things that you don't want her to see?" she says. "I understand him. I don't bother him; I leave him alone. But his Rat Pack, his Rat Pack goes down and enjoys."

The pack is tight-knit: Bell, college teammate Jerry Chang, Jagoda, sometimes Steinberg, assorted high school and college pals. It is, Woods says, "a lot easier than you'd think" for him to break free of his celebrity and enjoy himself. If you are outside the circle, no matter how long you've known him, he'll be polite, maybe even interested in what you have to say, but his supreme self-assurance ("If you truly love yourself," he says, "then obviously everything will be O.K.") can be

off-putting. Unless you're a member of the pack, spending time with Woods is like walking into a bank vault: It's shiny and cool and quiet, but after a while you realize there's no place to sit. Soon you find yourself edging toward the door, and he doesn't contest that move for a second.

It took a while, but Woods has fame sussed out. His first years on Tour, he says, "were like somebody threw me into the fire and said, 'Deal with it.' No one could've prepared me or anyone else for the type of life I've had to become accustomed to." His schedule was packed, he traveled to exhaustion, and he was the focus of every Tour stop. "What he went through for two years was devastating," says John Anselmo, Woods's swing coach for eight years when Tiger was a kid. "So much was demanded of him; everybody was making money off him, let's face it. It's different now."

Woods's non-Tour schedule has been pared to a minimum. He does a handful of clinics a year for kids. As he has cleared distractions from his game, he has become less volatile on the course. He allows himself to play. After his second round at the Nissan, Woods went to the range to work on his swing, and all around him were colleagues: Corey Pavin, Vijay Singh, Peter Jacobsen. All drove ball after ball into the dusk, but after a while Woods got distracted by the blinding spotlight mounted high up on the range fence, 40 yards away. He grabbed a sand wedge, turned and went to work, grinning at the game: One, two, three shots, each getting closer to the bulb. On his fourth try, the ball clanged off the light's housing. Two shots later he hit it again. He never stopped smiling.

He's as happy as he has ever been. "No doubt about it," Woods says, "I have a wonderful balance in my life. I've come to an understanding of what I need, what I can and can't do. I've learned what's best for me." He has learned partly because he has as stellar a pool of advisers as a young superstar could dream of, and he has given them an alphabet soup of nicknames: M (Jordan), J.R. (Ken Griffey Jr.), Mark-O (Meara). But in golf Woods values most the kinship he feels with Nicklaus. "We have an understanding of each other, just because of the way we play," Woods says. "The passion and the competitive drive we both have, it's inherent. I definitely sense something when I'm around him. We're a lot alike."

Told that Nicklaus had talked recently about their bond, Woods casually asks, "What'd he say?" When the conversation veers in a different direction, he grows more insistent. "What'd he say?"

It's a late March morning in Windermere, Fla., damp air heating up. Woods has been off for a week, but his usual spring allergies (yes, the holder of two Masters records is allergic to azaleas) have left him sniffly. He steps to the edge of a dock, hawks and spits into the lake. Isleworth, Windermere's gated enclave, is Woods's other refuge, the home, too, of O'Meara and Griffey, the place where he can fish and relax. Today he'll meet with the architects of the new house he's thinking about building here. He's been staying in a modest two-bedroom house he owns. "It's not what everyone has reported, this *mansion*," says Woods, shaking his head. "It's interesting. People know more about my life than I do."

Setting and price tag aside, Woods's lair is your classic postcollege crash pad. The Masters trophy sits amid the mess that is Woods's office desk. His living-room sofa holds a giant stuffed ape wearing an Afro wig. On this morning Woods dons the wig to answer the door and yelps, "I'm ready!" A photographer has come to snap his picture. Woods endures the invasion with charm and humor, pulling his pants up to his chest like Urkel, brushing his nonexistent bangs down and saying, like the character in the film *American Pie*, "Laid-back Tiger?" and then brushing them up, "Or cool-hip Tiger?" His cheapness is legendary: Pulling on one shirt brought by the photographer's stylist, he asks in all seriousness, "Do I get it free, or do I get a discount?"

Later, during a break, he sits on the edge of the dock staring at a spiderweb woven into a corner. Woods is a freak for nature shows; something in the Darwinian scramble for supremacy leaves him entranced. "How does the spider get from here to there?" he says. He stares some more, talks about the prey and how the spider weaves its trap thicker in the middle, sticky on some strands and dry on others. "Two different web secretions," Woods says. "It just knows which one to use. It's hereditary."

Tiger doesn't think much about life after golf. "This is a sport I could literally play for a lifetime," he says. Earl often declares that his son will be an agent of social change, but Tiger feels at home in the world of the rich and powerful. His views on gun control ("It's up to each and every person to do what he wants"), the shootings at Columbine High ("What we have forgotten is our values and morals and understanding of proper respect; a lot of kids aren't taught that"), race relations ("We're making progress slowly but surely") and the South Carolina Confederate flag flap ("I'm a golfer. That's their deal, you know?") make him fit for the Republican nomination. Don't expect a flurry of cage rattling anytime soon.

"It's pretty out here, isn't it?" Woods says, gazing across the still water. "You can tell it hasn't rained in a while. Look: The moss is all brown. Usually it's a little more green than this."

Still, spring is coming, and Augusta. He has been thinking about Augusta since New Year's. He has his father's voice ringing in his head, and he loves himself very much. Tiger Woods is ready to tee it up. This is his game now, and this is the man he has become. ●

THE TIGER SLAM

Chapter 3

2000-2001

2000 U.S. OPEN

Seeking the first leg of his slam, Tiger Woods teed off on the 14th hole during the third round at Pebble Beach.

TIGER WOODS

2000 U.S. OPEN

Tiger's third-round
71 gave him a
10-shot lead
heading into Sunday.

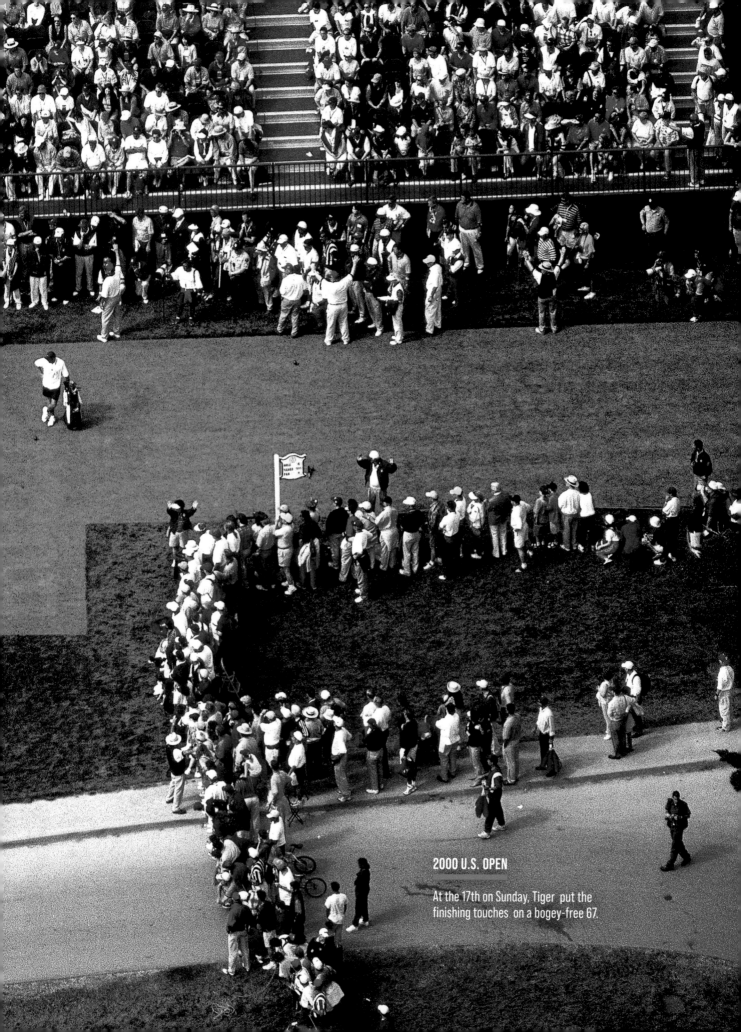

2000 U.S. OPEN

At the 17th on Sunday, Tiger put the finishing touches on a bogey-free 67.

Excerpted from Sports Illustrated, June 26, 2000

The 2000 U.S. Open

Tiger won at Pebble Beach by a record-breaking
15 strokes, as new swing improvements
elevated his game into the stratosphere

by JOHN GARRITY

Tiger Woods sees the world in narrow focus. Ball. Target. The space between. ESPN's Chris Berman walked up to him as Woods was hitting balls on the Pebble Beach practice range last Saturday, before the delayed start of the third round of the 100th U.S. Open, and tried to arrange an on-camera chat. Woods politely brushed him off. NBC course reporter Roger Maltbie asked Woods if he would take part in a preround interview. Woods said no.

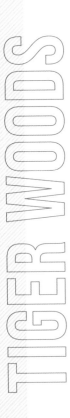

"They pay me the big bucks to ask you," Maltbie said with a smile.

Woods's expression said, They pay me the bigger bucks to say no.

Woods sees himself as an icon, one for the ages. That was evident in the stone-cold way that he went about winning his first U.S. Open and third major title, with the most dominating four-round performance in the history of major-championship golf. His winning margin was 15 strokes—two better than the record for a major set by Old Tom Morris at the 1862 British Open against a field of about a dozen—and his manner of winning was intimidating. Woods hit longer, straighter drives than anyone else. He flew iron shots that held on Pebble's small, firm greens. He never three-putted. This made even the most accomplished players look uncomfortable and unworthy. "Tiger has raised the bar," said Tom Watson, who won his only U.S. Open at Pebble Beach in 1982, "and it seems that he's the only guy who can jump over that bar."

That Tiger has raised his own standard by so much, while already the No. 1 golfer in the world, was the biggest revelation of this millennial Open. The extreme conditions of the layouts in past U.S. Opens have always exposed the holes in Woods's game. He was either a little too wild off the tee or lacked distance control from the fairway or didn't have a steady touch with the putter. But through his ceaseless work with his swing coach, Butch Harmon, he has mastered every shot in his deep arsenal.

If the goal is to beat the entire golf world into submission, Woods is practically there. In the last two years he has refined his game, and now he is the world's best driver of the ball, its best iron player, best chipper and best putter. But above all he is the game's most focused player. The week before the Open, he spent three days in Las Vegas with Harmon, and part of his preparation on the driving range at Rio Secco Golf Club involved simulating all the shots he would need at Pebble Beach. "We really didn't have to fix anything in Tiger's swing," said Harmon. "We just had to shape some shots, curve the ball a bit differently for some of the holes out there."

Still Tiger was not satisfied. On the eve of the Open, he spent extra time on the practice green at Pebble Beach even though he was putting superbly. "I didn't like the way I was rolling the ball," he said after his first-round 65, during which he needed just 24 putts. "I was making quite a few putts in practice rounds, but the ball wasn't turning over the way I would like to see it roll. I worked on it for a couple of hours and found that my posture was a little off. My release wasn't quite right." For the championship he took a total of only 110 putts, tied for sixth-best in the field.

His work ethic was the source of some controversy the day before the tournament when he skipped a ceremony honoring the late Payne Stewart, last year's Open champion, and instead chose to play a scheduled practice round. To those who criticized him for that decision he replied, "I felt going [to the cer-

His insurmountable lead turned Sunday's round into a Tigerfest.

emony] would be more of a deterrent for me during the tournament, because I don't want to be thinking about it." So much for sentiment in the march of history.

No less an authority on athletic intensity than NHL coach Scotty Bowman, who has won eight Stanley Cups, marveled at the single-mindedness of Woods's focus. Bowman walked the course with Tiger's twosome on Sunday as a USGA scorer and said, "His eye contact is right with his caddie and nowhere else when he's preparing to hit a shot. He's oblivious to everyone else."

The pursuit of perfection can be lonely, but in Woods's case it is not without passion. Even with a commanding seven-stroke lead on Saturday morning, when he hit his tee shot onto the rocks left of the 18th fairway, a microphone caught his sulfuric response. "I got a little angry and let the emotion get the better of me," he said later.

That fire was unquenchable even as he waltzed to victory. When the sun went down on the Monterey Peninsula on Sunday night, he held tournament records for the largest lead after 36 holes (six strokes), lowest 36-hole score (134, tied with Jack Nicklaus, T.C. Chen and Lee Janzen), largest 54-hole lead (10), lowest 72-hole score (272, tied with Nicklaus and Janzen), most strokes under par (12, tied with Gil Morgan, who reached that total in the third round in 1992, only to collapse and finish tied for 13th) and, of course, largest margin of victory.

Woods seemed merely to toy with and tease the Open field. In meddlesome third-round winds he made a triple bogey and a bogey on the front nine but still produced enough birdies to make the turn in par 35 and stretch his lead from six strokes to nine. Buried in a dense nest of grass atop the lip of a fairway bunker on the par-5 6th hole on Saturday, Woods still made birdie by punching his approach to 10 feet. Woods made practically every par-saving putt over four days, even the 15-footers. "He's playing every shot like his life depends on it," said Denmark's Thomas Bjorn, who played with Woods on Saturday.

By the time USGA president Trey Holland handed Woods the Championship Cup on Sunday afternoon, any doofus who still questions whether Woods is the world's best golfer was left to ponder these facts: Woods, at 24, has won a Masters by 12 strokes, a U.S. Open by 15 and a PGA Championship by a whisker. When he wins the British Open at St. Andrews in July, he will become just the fifth player—and the youngest by two years— to win all four majors. ("If he doesn't win the British Open," said recently retired Royal and Ancient secretary Sir Michael Bonallack,

"there should be a steward's inquiry.") And just to numb you with numbers, Woods has won 12 of his last 21 PGA Tour starts and this year has pocketed almost $5 million in prize money. "We always felt someone would come along who could drive the ball 300 yards and putt like Ben Crenshaw," Nick Price said after his round on Sunday. "This guy drives the ball farther than anybody I've ever seen and putts better than Crenshaw. He's a phenomenon."

The only brief insult to Woods's dignity came on the third hole of the third round, when he needed three swings from the greenside rough to get his ball onto the putting surface. The triple bogey so devastated Woods that he took, oh, 60 minutes to get his lead back to where it was. In the end he was light-years ahead of the runners-up, Ernie Els, the two-time U.S. Open champ from South Africa, and Miguel Angel Jimenez, the Ryder Cupper from Spain.

It was also a week of goodbyes. Besides the touching salute to Stewart, whose death in a plane crash last October kept him from defending the Open title he had won so dramatically a year ago at Pinehurst, there was the farewell to four-time U.S. Open champion Jack Nicklaus. Playing his 44th and final Open, on the course where in 1961 he won his second U.S. Amateur and in '72 his third U.S. Open, Nicklaus shot 73-82 and missed the cut.

The King is dead. Long live the King.

The rest of the Open belonged to Woods. You had Tiger making a 30-foot birdie putt on the 12th hole to close out play at dusk on Friday...Tiger hitting the ball on the rocks at 18 and turning the air blue...Tiger making his triple on number 3 without uttering a peep.... Tiger smiling and shaking his head after his miracle shot from the bunker lip at 6. You had Tiger, and, come to think of it, that's about all you had. When he teed off on Sunday afternoon, Woods enjoyed a 10-stroke lead and

" If the goal is to beat the entire golf world into submission, Woods is practically there. In the last two years he has refined his game, and now he is the world's best driver of the ball, its best iron player, best chipper and best putter. But above all he is the game's most focused player.

NBC had a television first: a 6½-hour telecast of exhibition golf. (Still the overnight ratings were up a glittering 11% from a year ago, further testament to Woods's popularity.)

Tiger reported to the 1st tee in a blood-red victory shirt and then bled off any possible drama by making nine consecutive pars in placid, sunny conditions. It wasn't until the back nine that he made his play for history. Woods birdied 10, 12, 13 and 14, taking his score to 12 under. On number 15 he flashed a desperate grimace over a perfectly decent tee shot that landed in the first cut of rough—a clear indication that he wanted to break records. Padraig Harrington, the Ryder Cupper from Ireland, said he paid no attention to what Woods was doing until he finished his own round. "But afterward," he admitted, "I looked at the scoreboard in total wonderment."

The microphones were still open when Woods stepped onto the 18th tee, but this time they picked up nothing but the solid click of his safe four-iron shot to the fairway. At the green he two-putted for par and a record-tying 272, hugged the principals, waved to the crowd and slipped three cigars out of his pocket, handing them to his girlfriend, Joanna Jagoda. Notably absent on Father's Day was his father, Earl Woods, who watched the tournament by himself at his home in Cypress, Calif. "The reason I didn't come up was that I wanted to give him the space to perform and be himself," Earl said. "It's all part of the plan."

His son had fogged the field on Thursday and strolled home in sunshine on Sunday, and by the time he was finished virtually no one was prepared to say that Nicklaus, Watson, Bobby Jones or anyone was in his league. The ultimate compliment came from the novelist and longtime golf writer Dan Jenkins, chronicler of the water-to-wine miracles of Ben Hogan. After watching Woods shoot four straight rounds of par or better on a course that had yielded only 32 subpar rounds by others, Jenkins said, "I saw him do things this week that I never saw Hogan do."

Hogan, of course, didn't approach perfection until he was in his late 30s. Tiger Woods has 22 more majors to compete in before he turns 30. Don't think that he doesn't know it. ●

Tiger Woods teed off on his Sunday round at St. Andrews, Scotland.

2000 BRITISH OPEN

2000 BRITISH OPEN

Tiger took the lead during
Round 2 and never relinquished
it, shooting 67-66-67-69 on the
par-72 Old Course.

2000 BRITISH OPEN

During the four days of
the tournament Woods
made 22 birdies and never
once landed in a bunker.

TIGER WOODS

Excerpted from SPORTS ILLUSTRATED, July 31, 2000

The 2000 British Open

With this win Tiger Woods completed a career
grand slam—which was both a rare feat and a prelude
for his greater accomplishment to come

by STEVE RUSHIN

Is Tiger ready?" David Duval asked on Sunday night, standing with his bags packed in front of the Old Course Hotel in St. Andrews, Scotland—the birthplace (and perhaps final resting spot) of golf. Three hours earlier Duval, the world's No. 2 player, was beaten, in ridiculous fashion, by Tiger Woods in the British Open, as were 71 other also-rans, and now, in the dark, Duval again deferred to the champion.

A private jet idled at Leuchars Royal Air Force base, five minutes away, a winged chariot that had been chartered by the agency that manages both Woods and Duval. It would fly the two men—the Open's final pairing—to Orlando, along with Australian pro Stuart Appleby. Of course, there was no need for anyone to leave for the air base until Woods appeared outside the hotel. While the plane would not hesitate to take off without Appleby, "it's not going anywhere," Appleby said, "without Tiger."

Even to those who are tired of Woods—who are Tiger-fatigued—what happened next was arresting. Woods emerged from the hotel with a totem under each arm: One was a symbol of his old-soul experience, the other of his unfathomable youth. In his right hand was the claret jug, awarded to the Open champion. In his left, a carry-on bag bearing a faded sticker of the cartoon character Cartman, from *South Park*. "Bye, Mom, I love you," said Woods, kissing his mother, Tida, at the curb. "I'll call you when I get back." With that, Woods and his girlfriend, Joanna Jagoda, disappeared into a courtesy van, leaving Mom, history, Hogan, Nicklaus, drama and whatever remained of competitive golf all standing at the curb, waving goodbye.

With his 19-under-par performance at the Old Course, Woods lapped the field by eight strokes, 35 days after winning the U.S. Open by 15. In doing so, he achieved a career Grand Slam at age 24, two years younger than Jack Nicklaus was when he did it. Golf has gone strictly Black-Thai, and it's no longer optional. Woods now holds the record for most strokes under par in the Masters, the U.S. Open and the British Open. Until three-putting the second green last Saturday, he had played 63 consecutive holes in major championship competition without making bogey. "He's the best who ever played," Mark Calcavecchia sighed on Sunday, "and he's 24."

How dramatically did Woods complete his reinvention of the game, on the site of its actual invention? Consider this watershed, remarkable for its sudden lack of remarkability: With Woods having won the the PGA, the U.S. Open and the British Open and Vijay Singh having won the Masters, it has been more than a year since a white guy won a major championship. St. Andrews may be the home of golf, but Woods has become the game's absentee owner. "Somebody out there," said Thomas Bjorn, who tied for sec-

ond last week with Ernie Els, "is playing golf on a different planet."

In fact, the entire field at St. Andrews played on the cratered surface of the moon. The Old Course's famous bunkers—essentially uncovered manholes—were steepened further for the millennial Open. If that news wasn't ominous enough, an attendant bearing a seven-foot rake followed each group, like Death with his scythe. On Sunday, Duval took four strokes to get out of the Road Hole bunker on 17, the infamous Sands of Nakajima, as the Grim Raker discreetly averted his gaze. Woods likewise looked away.

Earlier in the week Calcavecchia and Sergio García had both putted away from the six-foot-high wall of that bunker before even attempting to pitch out. Tsuyoshi Yoneyama blasted out backward, toward the tee box. But Woods, almost embarrassingly, played 72 holes on a course with 112 bunkers and never soiled his trouser cuffs. Given the 10 pieces of luggage that he and Jagoda carried to Scotland, he could afford to have done so. "He brought everything," said his mother, "except kitchenware."

But then, Woods demands order and routine at the majors. For four days he is afflicted

> **He achieved a career Grand Slam at age 24, two years younger than Jack Nicklaus was when he did it. Golf has gone strictly Black-Thai, and it's no longer optional.**

with a kind of tournament Tourette's, exhibiting countless obsessive compulsions. In practice he sometimes requires himself to hole 100 six-foot putts. Consecutively. Using only his right hand. He also barks the odd obscenity after tee shots, as he did last Thursday after pulling a ball into the rough on 17.

He's a neat freak who picks lint off greens with the fastidiousness of Felix Unger. He turned his back to the gallery on most fairways last week to honk into his hanky or apply eyedrops with a Poindexterous proficiency. For just under the surface of Woods's Nike-baked glaze remains a golf wonk named Eldrick: When they were teammates at Stanford, Notah Begay called the allergy-addled, dickie-wearing freshman Urkel.

Yet for all his manifold tics—the honking and sneezing and barking—Woods goes plac-

Tiger celebrated earning his first Claret Jug.

id as a Zen garden before hitting a golf ball. That is his physical genius. "All players have some preshot routine," says Nick Faldo, the next iciest golfer of the last 15 years, whose British Open low-aggregate record Woods broke at St. Andrews. "Tiger has blitzed all that. There's no twitch, no lift of the hat, no wasted energy."

A tournament-record throng of 230,000 attended this year's Open, and it finally overwhelmed Her Majesty's Marshals on Sunday evening, breaching the security cordon on the 18th fairway and pouring forth behind Woods like water through a burst dam, threatening to carry him to the green. Security guards who had evidently cut their teeth on soccer hooligans pitched at least two spectators into the Swilken Burn, the creek that runs across the 1st and 18th fairways.

When Woods finally reached his tee shot on 18, a comprehensively tanned woman, wearing but a tattoo, gamboled from the gallery to the green, where she grabbed the flag and danced around it as if it were a maypole. Just like that, half of Scotland looked like Tiger—wearing scarlet on Sunday. Inside the 146-year-old Royal & Ancient clubhouse, monocles fell into soup tureens. When a policeman finally bundled the streaker from sight, Woods chipped on and two-putted. His world domination was complete. Thus was ushered in the Leaden Age of Sportswriting.

For what will be left to say of Woods's golf game five years, five months, five weeks from now? "He has to have challengers for the whole thing to be right," Nicklaus told a tentful of scribes last week. "It's a bad story if there aren't any challengers. You guys won't have anything to write about."

Indeed, last weekend saw the final pages flipped on some cosmic Chinese golf calendar—from the Age of the Bear to the Age of the Tiger. When Nicklaus putted out on 18 on Friday, ending what is presumed to have been his final round ever at the British, Woods happened to be 50 yards away, near the 1st tee, practicing his putting in advance of his own round.

Woods may have learned too well from Nicklaus, whose records were taped to the headboard of Tiger's bed even at age 10. Of his list of achievements, Woods actually said on Sunday night, "I thought I'd be at this point faster than it took," which is to say sooner. With such ambitions, victory results not in joy but relief. Woods's smile, while famous, is far too infrequent. More often he wears the game face: It could serve as a gargoyle on the gray granite buildings of St. Andrews. He doesn't save his game face strictly for the golf course, either. Woods and Mark O'Meara spent the week before the British Open playing golf and fly-fishing in Ireland. O'Meara caught a six-pound Atlantic salmon one morning after Woods had slipped off to eat breakfast. When Tiger returned to see the fish, his face betrayed something other than delight. "I could tell," says O'Meara, "he wished it had been him who caught it."

So it is with majors. Woods wants all the fish worth catching, and he intends to take his limit. Things could be worse for his colleagues: Colin Montgomerie has become wealthy winning 24 nonmajors, nine of them named for car manufacturers. "I'll go on doing what I do, winning the Volvo PGAs," he said last week, staring into a bland, if lavishly automotive, future. Likewise Ernie Els. Or rather, Ernie Ls: He has finished second to Woods four times—this year. "Everybody," says Nicklaus, "has thrown up the white flag and surrendered." Then again, says Calcavecchia, "If Jack was in his prime today, I don't think he could keep up with Tiger."

Is it any wonder, then, that Montgomerie snapped, "Next question," when Woods's name was raised in the interview tent last week? Els was asked to talk about Woods 45 seconds into his session with the press after taking the first-round lead. "C'mon, that's not fair," said the Big Easy, uneasily. "I just shot a 66. If you want to talk to Tiger, call him on the telephone."

Good luck getting through. "Gods do not answer letters," John Updike wrote of Ted Williams, who refused to tip his cap after homering in his final at bat at Fenway. Woods, another athletic prodigy who sounds as if he's no fun to fish with, doesn't take phone calls. He has his circle of friends, but most adhere to a strict code of omerta—or is it a code of O'Meara?—that ensures the public will never likely get to know him. Which is fine, because his performances will more than suffice as entertainment. "Why does the writing make us chase the writer?" the British novelist Julian Barnes wrote of the modern obsession with celebrity. "Why aren't the books enough?"

One only hopes that Woods can enjoy his feats as much as others do. When Justin Leonard, briefly a contender to Tiger's generational supremacy, won the British Open at Troon in 1997, he sneaked back onto the course at midnight and drank champagne on the 18th green. While Woods left St. Andrews in his jetwash well before the clock struck 12 on Sunday, he did celebrate in a small way, a way that suggests he might one day loosen up, maybe even undo the top button of his polo shirt.

Before leaving town, he ducked into a building on the grounds of the Old Course and said thank you to the tournament committee. He posed for pictures while flustered staffers struggled to work their Instamatics. Finally, claret jug in his left hand, he raised a glass of champagne with his right. Said Woods, "I'd like to make a toast to St. Andrews."

The new and future champion took a small sip, grimaced a small smile and, another duty done, politely began to make his exit. But his girlfriend wouldn't have it. "Keep drinking!" Jagoda ordered. Woods, dutifully, emptied the flute. ●

2000 PGA CHAMPIONSHIP

Tiger exulted after draining a birdie putt on the first playoff hole.

2000 PGA

Tiger made this birdie putt on the 18th hole to qualify for the playoff against May.

2000 PGA

Above: Tiger and Jack Nicklaus were paired together in the opening rounds.
Right: On Sunday Tiger hit a recovery shot on the second playoff hole.

Excerpted from SPORTS ILLUSTRATED, August 28, 2000

The 2000 PGA Championship

For the third leg of his slam, Tiger needed to rally to
make a playoff against a surprising challenge from a
journeyman playing the tournament of his life

by ALAN SHIPNUCK

Late on Sunday evening Tiger Woods and his processional
toured the grounds of Valhalla Golf Club, attending to some
of the obligations that come with making history. Champagne
was poured, presentations made and everywhere Woods
went he was fussed over as if he were a visiting pasha.

One PGA Championship official shadowed Woods's every move, his only duty being to lug around the oversized Wanamaker Trophy, which Woods had retained for another year by successfully defending his title earlier in the day. Another minion was serving him food, including a plate of cantaloupe and pineapple, a serving of rice and a strawberry Popsicle, all of which Woods scarfed down as he floated from one function to the next.

Amidst the pomp and circumstance Woods wore his usual superstar sheen, his omnipresent smile like an endless row of piano keys, but as soon as he hit the parking lot, something changed. Away from the bright lights and fawning fans his star power seemed to drain away. By the time Woods made the long walk across the parking lot to a wait-

ing stretch limousine, he was walking with a pronounced limp. "My calf is killing me," he groaned, referring to soreness in his right leg. Settling into the limo, the weight of the world seemed to finally hit him. "Man, I'm tired," Woods said before disappearing into the night. "It's been a long day."

To see a spent and suffering Woods was to be reminded that he's still flesh and blood, a fact all but obscured by the otherworldly golf he had played over the final day of the PGA. Pushed to the brink by fearless 31-year-old journeyman Bob May, Woods responded with the most clutch performance of an already legendary career. Trailing by two strokes early in the final round, he played the last 12 regulation holes in seven under par to force a three-hole playoff and then won the trophy with a birdie and a pair of bloodless pars.

This was golf to raise the dead, and as Woods's dominance continues, it has become increasingly apparent that he's competing only against the ghosts of the game's greats. For Woods, this PGA was his third victory by a record-low score in a major championship in the past nine weeks, following wins by unprecedented margins at the U.S. and British Opens. He now joins Ben Hogan as the only other player to prevail in three professional majors during a season. Hogan's hat trick, in 1953, has always ranked along Byron Nelson's '45 campaign, when Nelson won 18 tournaments, including 11 in a row, as the standards by which a standout season is measured. For nearly half a century none of these performances has been matched, and now, suddenly, these benchmark years all have been surpassed by Woods in 2000. With the thunder of his PGA victory still echoing, it's time to put into words what Woods has said so eloquently with his clubs: He has wrought the greatest season in golf history.

"Someday I'll tell my grandkids I played in the same tournament as Tiger Woods," Hall of Famer Tom Watson said. "We are witnessing a phenomenon here that the game may never, ever see again."

On Sunday, May played like a champion. Woods played like a god, albeit one who got off to a slow start. When he three-putted the 6th hole for his second bogey of the day, Woods found himself in a four-way tie for second, two in arrears of May, who was rousing the specter of Jack Fleck. Woods rallied with consecutive birdies on 7 and 8 to pull even with May, and a back nine for the ages ensued.

On the par-5 10th both players got up-and-down from the sand for birdie. On 11, May sank a 25-foot bomb for a

Woods would finish the second round at -11, while May lurked at -6.

birdie that propelled him back into the lead. At 12, a brutal 467-yard par-4 that is Valhalla's number 1 handicap hole, May stuffed an eight-iron from 181 yards to two feet for his third straight birdie. Warming to the chase, Woods drilled a 15-footer to stay one down. Both played brilliant shots into the par-3 14th, and Woods holed his downhill, sidehill 15-foot putt. May stepped up and topped him with a tricky 12-footer. How long could the perfect golf continue? "That was an incredible battle," Woods said. "We never backed off. Birdie for birdie, shot for shot, that's as good as it gets."

The drama heightened at the par-4 15th. May striped a seven-iron to within six feet of the cup, while Woods pulled his approach to the left and played an indif-

TIGER WOODS

ferent putt from off the green. It looked like May might go three strokes ahead with three holes to play. Still away, Woods then buried a big-breaking 15-footer to save par. "I knew if I made mine, it would make his putt a little bit longer," Woods said later, and sure enough, May blew his birdie chance, his first stumble.

Woods finally drew even with a textbook birdie on 17, and on 18, an uphill par-5 of 542 yards, both reached the saddle-shaped green with two mighty blows, setting up long, difficult lag putts. May went first, from the front left, and his nerve momentarily deserted him. He blasted his putt clear off the green, 15 feet above the hole, and when Tiger putted to within six feet, it looked as if the fight might be over. But then May brushed in his ball with alarming ease, and suddenly Woods needed a knee-knocking downhill six-footer to prevent an upset that would haunt him for the rest of his career. Once again, he willed his ball into the cup. "That's why he's Tiger Woods," said May.

The ensuing three-hole playoff seemed anticlimatic, especially after Woods rolled in a 20-footer on the first extra hole, the 16th, to take his first lead since the 2nd hole. Woods's finger-wagging celebration following his birdie may have been the most animated of his career. He held on to the lead with a scrappy par on 17—out of the rough, off a cart path and into a drainage area. At 18, Woods got up-and-down from the front bunker to seal the win.

Woods's and May's four-round totals of minus 18 broke the PGA Championship standard of minus 17 set by Steve Elkington and Colin Montgomerie in 1995, meaning Woods owns or co-owns the scoring record in all four majors. More mind-blowing: Were it not for one bad three-hole stretch in April, we could be enjoying a new Spike Lee movie, *Summer of Slam*. During the first round of the Masters, Woods double-bogeyed the 10th hole—his approach shot plugging in the greenside bunker—and then tripled the

short, dangerous par-3 12th hole, when his eight-iron shot got caught up in the swirling breeze, landed on the bank short of the green and trickled into Rae's Creek. In the span of three holes he dropped five strokes to par, but with steady play the rest of the way, he finished fifth, six strokes behind winner Vijay Singh.

Woods's unprecedented play in the majors this year is what gives his season the nod over those of Jones, Nelson and Hogan. Jones's Grand Slam was vastly different from the modern Slam. Sure, he won the U.S. and British Opens, but he didn't have to face the era's top professionals in victories at the U.S. and British Amateurs. As for Nelson's storied year, he won only the one major that was played that year (the PGA), as the Masters and the U.S. and British Opens were all canceled because of World War II. The fact that Nelson was 4-F because of a blood condition meant that he faced thin fields throughout his record season. (For example, U.S. Army Air Corps Captain Hogan wasn't discharged until August 1945.) In his signature season Hogan won his three majors by a combined 15 strokes, or put another way, Woods's margin of victory at this year's U.S. Open.

Woods's mastery has extended far beyond the majors. He has seven victories this year. He's also on his way to shattering one of the game's most hallowed records. In golf, the equivalent of Ted Williams's .406 batting average in '41 has been Sam Snead's season-scoring record of 69.23, set in 1950. Woods's scoring average is now 68.59.

At the U.S. Open, Woods didn't have a three-putt; at the British Open he didn't hit a single bunker. With both Pebble Beach and the Old Course playing hard and fast, his victories were models of precision and restraint. At Valhalla, with its generous fairways and receptive greens, Woods clubbed the par-5s into submission, birdieing all four on Thursday by reaching the greens with a seven-iron, a seven-iron, a four-iron and a seven-iron. "My gosh, he hits the ball a long way," Nicklaus said, sounding like a man who had finally found religion.

Saturday seemed ripe for Woods to turn on the afterburners. When a storm blew through in the wee hours of Friday morning, dumping more than three inches of rain, suddenly the fairways were soft and receptive, and the greens downright marshmallowy. Saturday also brought easier pin placements, and the birdies flew fast and furious.

Though his swing was out of sync early in the third round, Woods scraped around brilliantly, and at the 10th hole he was four under on the day and three shots clear of the field. But he had flown too high on borrowed wings. His shaky ball striking finally caught up with him at 12, where he took a stunning double bogey that trimmed his lead to one over his plucky playing partner, Scott Dunlap. Woods took another bogey at 15, pulling a six-iron 40 yards left into the cabbage. With a clutch two-putt birdie at 18 he regained sole possession of the lead, one ahead of May and Dunlap, who would fade on Sunday with a 75.

So the final round came, and Woods and May had the chance to renew acquaintances.

They had grown up 20 minutes apart in Southern California, back in the days when Woods wasn't the only prodigy. Nearly every Sunday morning for six years, from the time Bob was 11, his parents would schlepp him clear across the Los Angeles basin, from their middle-class neighborhood in La Habra to the rarefied air of Bel-Air Country Club, where Bob had a standing 7 a.m. lesson with Bel-Air's legendary Eddie (Li'l Pro) Merrins. It's unusual for an outsider to be accorded such a welcome at Bel-Air, but Merrins saw something special in May, who would more than fulfill the promise. At 16 he played his way into the L.A. Open, becoming the youngest competitor in the tournament's history (a distinction Woods usurped by a few months, when he was 16). May so dominated the junior golf scene in Southern California that Woods, seven years his junior, says now, "I just wanted to hopefully one day win as many tournaments as he did."

Bob May, take heart. Yours are hardly the only records that Woods has smashed as he continues to overwhelm golf's notions of the impossible. •

"Someday I'll tell my grandkids I played in the same tournament as Tiger Woods," Hall of Famer Tom Watson said. "We are witnessing a phenomenon here that the game may never, ever see again."

Excerpted from SPORTS ILLUSTRATED, December 18, 2000

2000 Sportsman of the Year

Three quarters of the way through his Slam and still
only 24 years old, Tiger Woods had arguably become
bigger than the game he was dominating

by FRANK DEFORD

MUSICAL INTERLUDE: Trumpets and flourishes
INTERVIEW LOCATION: A franchise pro shop in Malltown, USA

Sure we love Tiger Woods. We adore him. He da man. But enough. What about the fans who support the Game—us, the Worldwide Gallery?

What are we going to do about him? Is there a certain point at which he starts to ruin things for us, when he gets so good it's boring? We have to think about this. Has anybody in any sport been this much better than everyone else? Maybe the Babe when he was hitting more home runs than whole teams. But that's the point: He wasn't the whole damn team. He couldn't control the game on his own. Maybe Joe Louis, when every month the best they could do was dredge up a new palooka. Maybe the Great One, maybe Michael. But, hell, even Michael wasn't that much better than Magic or Bird. Tiger is alone. Before this year we thought he might be "the next Jordan." No

longer. The way we see it now, it is Jordan who is "the previous Woods."

Tiger's old man said Tiger was going to be Gandhi. Wrong. Gandhi was special, sure. But Buddha and St. Francis of Assisi, Martin Luther King...all in the Gandhi mix. A better analogy: Tiger is da Vinci. Nah, scratch that. Good as da Vinci was, he had Michelangelo at his shoulder, No. 2 with a bullet. Robin Hood had William Tell, Beethoven had Mozart, Oprah has Martha. But Tiger? He's all alone; nobody else in his line of work has ever been on the same fairway.

Maybe we bought into him too fast. After all, we made Nicklaus earn our affection. We even resented him at first. Fat Jack. Remember that? Tiger? He is the American Prince William. We watched him grow up, waiting lovingly for him to take the throne. Has an athlete ever been so ordained? Then he not only lives up to our expectations but also tops our impossible dreams. Tiger Woods, dream beater.

So what fun is that? How many times can we depend on somebody named Bob May to catch lightning in Jack Fleck's bottle? We're all rooting for Tiger to win every major by 17 strokes, to win every tournament in the Northern Hemisphere. (Is Thailand in the Southern Hemisphere? Whatever.) Yes, absolutely, we are into excellence, but we have to admit that deep in our dark souls most every one of us now longs for the day when the kid misses a cut or shoots an 80 or even pulls a Van de Velde. Just once, humbled. Do you know, in the London betting shops, he is 3-2 to win the Masters next April and 16-1 to sweep the Grand Slam? Excuse us: Only 16-1 on what was inconceivable.

We are not mean-spirited, you understand. We love Tiger Woods. It is only that we are human, and you need human stuff on the golf course. Otherwise it all becomes one of those standard golf jokes in which Moses and St. Peter and Mohammed are trading miracles in a five-buck Nassau. Has Tiger made that a foursome?

MUSICAL INTERLUDE: A sample of the sappiest of the Mantovani-type fluff played by all networks on their golf telecasts
INTERVIEW LOCATION: Media bar, Sunbelt.com Open

Oh, we're supposed to go on even more about Tiger for your benefit? Give us a rest, us poor, put-upon Members of the Golfing Fourth Estate who chronicle the Game. It is not our problem that you star-kissers at SPORTS ILLUSTRATED are making him Sportsman of the Year. Again. What are you going to do when he wins the Grand Slam next year?

Retire the trophy? Well, join the party. We've got to genuflect in newsprint and on the air most every week.

It's getting harder, too, to spin anything original. Unfortunately for us journalists, the piece Charlie Pierce did on him in *GQ* in '97 spooked Tiger. Pierce described him as telling sophomoric dirty jokes and doing Buckwheat accents, the way most normal college kids do. That, however, didn't jibe with orthodox Tiger Woods theology, so, after that, he pretty much took the sports version of omerta. Now he presents himself as equal parts cliché and politeness. The guy who always goes for the pin keeps the world an arm's length from his heart.

In fact, it's almost as if we feel a compulsion to protect him. Tiger made only two public mistakes in 2000. Number 1: He was heard cursing on television after he hit a bad drive at the U.S. Open. Number 2: He filmed a commercial for Buick even though the Screen Actors Guild, of which he is a member, was on strike against commercial producers. The vulgarity was a trifling gaffe—and spontaneous and natural—while his defiance of his union was a calculated decision that was constructed of hubris and greed.

Yet most of us Tiger correspondents made a terrible fuss about the silly boo–boo—ohhh, Jack would never utter a profanity on a hallowed golf course; my, my, Michael was always above such coarseness—while little was made of the disregard for his union and its members. Then again, golf is not exactly hearth and home to the labor movement, and we who cover the game do it more gently than do our brethren who lurk about sweatier athletic venues, where azaleas never bloom.

Tiger is such an extraordinary champion and so widely admired that we have granted him a sort of spiritual amnesty. His persona is still insulated by his deeds, his misjudgments immunized by his youth. Sometime

TIGER WOODS

soon, though, we will weary of the tedium of his persistent success and start peering more deeply into that heavenly smile and beyond those steely eyes. Won't we? Because that's the nature of the beast—us. This, right now, may be the best Tiger will ever have it. Until, that is, he becomes a Grand Old Man, and we fall in love with him again.

MUSICAL INTERLUDE: Broadway medley of "Bosom Buddies" from *Mame*; "[You Gotta Have] Heart" from *Damn Yankees*; "A Hymn to Him" from *My Fair Lady*; "March of the Siamese Children" from *The King and I*; and "I'm Only Thinking of Him" from *Man of La Mancha*
INTERVIEW LOCATION: Practice tee, Tiger Woods commercial shoot

Don't even talk to us about him. Please, think about our feelings, have a heart for us other guys on the PGA Tour—we, the Members of the Professional Golfers Anonymous Tour, who make the Game.

People used to talk about how poor Colin Montgomerie hadn't won a major. The way things are going, we're all going to be Col-in-ized. Tiger, though, has made it worth our while to be spear carriers. Since it became the Tiger Tour, our prize money has tripled and our TV contracts have doubled. That means more exposure (at least for the lucky donkeys among us who get to play a round with him), which means more money for our endorsement contracts, too. Everybody can't be Buddy Holly. Somebody has to be the Crickets.

Are we envious? Sure, we are human. The skinny kid comes on the Tour, he's already famous—as an amateur. But he's good. He can hit it a continental mile. Then he gets to be No. 1, and he redoes his game and his body. On the Everest summit, sans oxygen, he performs a makeover. This is not fair. From 140 or 145 pounds, now he's packing 190, all muscle. Cut us a break.

Plus he's only 24. What happens when he hits his peak? Everybody says, What's the matter with you wimps? Why can't you challenge him? Hey, tell it to the Marines. Maybe the golfer who'll finally take out Tiger hasn't been born yet.

Listen to this: "When he plays well, he wins. When he plays badly, he finishes second. When he plays terrible, he finishes third." Guess who? Wrong. That's Johnny Miller talking about Nicklaus in 1973. Miller is a whiner. He didn't know how lucky he and his bunch were. Tiger only plays great, greater, greatest. The sonuvabitch is relentless, too. The same jackasses we have to put up with every week who scream "you da man" say he can only beat himself. As if it were the truth of the ages. Yeah, O.K., occasionally some young hotshot comes along who wins a lot and then acquires the entourage and the big head. Our problem is that the more Tiger wins, the less he lets up on himself.

MUSICAL INTERLUDE: Handel's Hallelujah Chorus
INTERVIEW LOCATION: The heavens above St. Andrews

I've been waiting here, laddie. It's about time you heard me out, because all these other chaps are just so many blowhards, and they've all got an ax to grind, haven't they? But you're here at the sacred place, and, Shhh! Let me speak, for I am the Game.

Nobody is bigger than the Game. Oh they do love to trot out that bromide, don't they? Especially the tired old blue blazers who have a vested interest in the proceedings. But I am the Game, remember, so I don't have to be literal. I can be lyrical. Right now your Mr. Woods is bigger than I am. Do not be shocked. Sometimes—and ever so happily— our institutions are, for a moment in time, overwhelmed by an extraordinary human talent. 'Twas always so. Was not Joan of Arc

TIGER WOODS

"

This, right now, may be the best Tiger will ever have it. Until, that is, he becomes a Grand Old Man, and we fall in love with him again.

bigger than War, Shakespeare bigger than the Stage, the Beatles bigger than Music?

At times, to be perfectly honest, I would rather be Wrestling than Golf. I find that endeavor curiously refreshing and so ingenious. Tradition can be so overbearing. As I was telling Atlas only last summer: One more hallowed reference to Old Tom Morris or the claret jug or Amen Corner and I think I'll scream. Here are those self-appointed sentinels of Golf complaining that young Mr. Woods is bringing in the wrong sort to our courses. Please: A bit of noise and joy will surely do us no real harm. And how grand it is that so many ladies and gentlemen of color are teeing up. Heavens, I understand that now there are a third again more African-Americans playing in the U.S.

Oh, gracious me, I was so sympathetic toward the young bloke last month when he ventured the most modest grievances about how the PGA Tour exploits him. Certainly he should be accorded special consideration—with hosannas! But there were those supercilious critics who cried out, Ah, where would Tiger be without the PGA Tour? I reported that to Atlas, and he screeched. (It would surprise you, but Atlas—not unlike

your Nicklaus and that brutish Mike Tyson—has an uncommonly high voice for such a strong fellow.) He positively shrieked to me, "That is like saying, Where would Alexander be without Persia?"

I do look forward to a siesta of especially long duration. Before my envious friend Atlas was saddled with holding up the sky, he had what you would now call a p.r. man, a Greek named Hesiod. To be sure, Hesiod was no Tiger Woods of poetry, no Homer, but still a man of considerable gifts—a Jones, a Hogan, I would say. Atlas told me that Hesiod wrote this: "Badness you can get easily, in quantity: The road is smooth, and it lies close by. But in front of excellence the immortal gods have put sweat, and long and steep is the way to it, and rough at first. But when you come to the top, then it is easy, even though it is hard."

I believe that wisdom applies perfectly to young Tiger Woods. He will continue to overcome what is hard, so that he might, with ease—and with my benediction—long carry the burden of being bigger than the Game. Now, if you will excuse me, since at last I find myself at leisure, I should rather like to play a round. Would you please thank Tiger for affording me that splendid opportunity? ●

On the precipice of history, Tiger drove from the 18th tee on Sunday at Augusta National.

2001 MASTERS

2001 MASTERS

Tiger lined up a putt during the opening round, in which he shot a 70.

TIGER WOODS

2001 MASTERS

Tiger shot a 68 on Saturday which, following his 66 on Friday, gave him the 54-hole lead.

Excerpted from Sports Illustrated, April 16, 2001

The 2001 Masters

By the time Tiger Woods completed his unprecedented
quartet with a win at Augusta, he had succeeded in
turning the unprecedented into the expected

by RICHARD HOFFER

It all felt preordained, inevitable, uneventful even. There wasn't a doubt in the world how this would play out. When it was over, not even the crowd, communicating the tournament's ups and downs through Augusta's acoustic hollows, could muster a truly surprised roar. Tiger Woods holed a 15-footer on 18, won the Masters by two strokes, completed a sweep of the four majors and generally made history.

The crowd exited with proper restraint, observing posted signs that said no running (but walking pretty fast all the same), to get home for dinner. There was hardly a sense that the moment ought to be savored or examined. Wasn't he just going to do this again next year?

It's come to this, then: A 25-year-old golfer has made victory in a major so routine that, even in the unthinkable stringing together of four of them, he is denied proper celebration. It will be argued that what he did, beginning with last year's U.S. Open instead of the Masters (he took a mulligan—so what?), is not really a Grand Slam, as if the term will be degraded to nothing more than a breakfast order if the majors aren't won in a calendar year. But, geez, if winning just one in a career were that easy, then people wouldn't root so hard for the game's second- and third-best golfers, Phil Mickelson and David Duval, who keep finishing runner-up, on their good days.

Only Woods seemed fully aware of what he'd achieved, and that realization suffered a little time lag. You may have seen it, only not recognized its import: Woods, the tournament in hand after Duval and Mickelson had bogeyed 16, was putting the finishing touches on Sunday's 68, hitting his tee shot 330 yards,

pitching 75 and then sinking his birdie try. "It was a great putt," said Woods, reconstructing the moment. "It went in, so be it. Then I walked over to the side, and I started thinking, I don't have any more shots to play. I'm done. I just won the Masters." Then he lost it a little and, lest that famous corporate composure be seen to crumble, covered his face with his cap, pulling it together in time to congratulate Mickelson after his two-putt.

It was the only glimpse of his raw desire that Woods allowed last week. Others, like the majorless Mickelson, admitted to "desperately" wanting the Masters. Mickelson, a bold player whose big bets on the golf course sometimes backfire (unlike his wagers in Las Vegas, where he turned $20,000 into a reported $560,000 betting on the Baltimore Ravens to win the Super Bowl), was unwisely naked in his ambition, although he responded to the pressure with three sub-70 rounds (67-69-69) that put him in the familiar position of facing off against Woods. (He's 2-1 in shootouts with Tiger.) Woods, meanwhile,

was characteristically coy, complaining of "plodding" rounds of 70-66-68, in which his shots were "fatted" or "bleeders" or otherwise unworthy of further discussion. "Grinding" was how he described his round on Sunday.

This self-deprecation, irritating early in his career when his so-called B game was blowing pretty good golfers out of the water, has become part of his patter. He employs it as reverse braggadocio, making it palatable with winks and grins. What it does, though, is mask the brutal concentration he brings to the game, so intense it doesn't even allow him to realize when he's done for the day. "When you are focused so hard on each and every shot," he says, "you kind of forget everything else."

This intensity is only growing. The nine wins last year and the three in a row this year (after a "slump" in which he failed to win any of eight tournaments) do not signal a golfer satisfied with himself. Woods and his father, Earl, who met at Tiger's home in Orlando for the trip to Augusta, immediately parted ways upon arrival and did not speak again until Sunday,

> **Let the DiMarcos of the world have their fun on Thursday and Friday because, underlying each event, there is the inevitability of Woods, picking up strokes here and there until it's over. "He seems to do just what is required," said Mickelson, "and I think if I had made a run [on Sunday], he may have followed suit."**

following that last birdie putt. "He was locked in," says Earl. Tiger instead holed up in a house with fellow pro and neighbor Mark O'Meara, reheating dinners that O'Meara's wife, Alicia, had prepared earlier in the week and avoiding all contact with the real world.

If you were persistent, you might have caught sight of him on the practice range, where he would repair after each round, pound balls into the twilight and then scoot away in his courtesy car. The car would be brought to the front of the clubhouse, Woods would slide into the driver's seat, and right before accelerating out the drive, he'd loll his head back against the seat, as if in sudden and complete nervous collapse. Then he'd be gone into the darkness. Or late on Sunday you might have seen tournament chairman Hootie Johnson ushering Woods into the clubhouse for the champion's dinner—"Don't worry, this won't take long," Johnson said—and Woods sagging against the wall, as if shot, saying, "I'm a little under the weather."

It could be that it's not so easy being Tiger Woods, though he makes many protestations to the contrary. "You think I'm lying," he said after Sunday's round, "but I actually felt more relaxed this week." He works hard behind the scenes at being the real Tiger Woods, however, developing and practicing shots on the off-chance he might need something special for Augusta.

Take Sunday's tee shot on 13, what he called a high sweeper. "I've practiced on the range all week just in case I might need it," he said. He didn't for three days as he played safely on the par-5, dogleg left. Come Sunday, with only a two-stroke lead on Mickelson, "I had to pull it out. I had to step up and aim another 15 yards farther right and hit that big slinger around the corner to give myself a chance." He birdied the hole to stay two-up. Another trick up his sleeve.

This sort of recourse has to be more discouraging than the field lets on. Woods, however, can tease the competition with his vulnerability, and let's face it, it has been four years since he turned pro and last won the Masters. This time, with the course yielding plenty of birdies and with Woods looking beatable earlier in the season, anybody seemed to have a chance. Wonderful scores were coming in through two rounds, and the leaderboard looked very interesting.

Still, everybody seemed to recognize that a timetable was at work, that a point would come when Woods's major machinery would be set in motion. Sure enough, Woods rose to the top for Sunday's show, but six golfers were within three shots of his lead. The Mickelson pairing was tantalizing, not only because Mickelson is one of those greatest-golfers-never-to-have-won-a-major, but also because of his luck in Tiger duels.

Woods used the 16th green to shake off Mickelson, who was gaining momentum. Mickelson barely missed a birdie putt of 35 feet, but it rolled seven feet past. He flubbed

Photographers asked Woods and Singh for multiple takes at the jacket ceremony.

the return for a bogey, while Woods made par. Who didn't see this coming?

If the tournament seemed to lack suspense, even with the game's three best golfers flailing at each other to the end, it was entertaining enough. Educational might be a better word. The first three days, as they often do, drew the curtains aside for a peek into the real world of golf, in which a less dignified desperation governs the field and folks scrabble for lost swings, new grips, an old peace of mind—anything to make a cut or just stay on Tour.

Chris DiMarco was the first to bring golf's underworld to the fore, cruising to a 65 and a Day One lead, stubbornly holding it into Saturday and then going shot-for-shot (more or less) with Woods in round 3.

Rocco Mediate, who shot 66 on Saturday to make a surprise appearance on the leaderboard, was another rehab project, resurrecting his game some years ago with a chin-high putter. Mark Calcavecchia, who was runner-up at the Masters in 1988 and hardly in contention at Augusta since, had a 66 on Friday and a 68 on Saturday, climbing to within two shots of Tiger.

A stranger to golf, seeing these three together on a putting green, might be excited by the possibilities of reinvention (whereas a purist would be horrified by the collective lack of form). It turns out that, with enough imagination, you can come back.

The tournament also reminded us of the generational divide that separates, roughly, Tiger's era from everybody else's. More to the point, that divide means about 20 extra yards off the tee. "The players today," said O'Meara, sounding much older than 44, "hit the ball so much farther and have such a big advantage." For 2002 the club intends to strengthen the defenses of some par-4s with extra yardage, although that would seem to reward Woods, longest off the tee through the tournament, rather than punish him.

The message, above all, is that Woods mocks the field with his talent and youth, and the only way to halfway keep up is to cobble together odd grips or layouts. Yet for all that, he did not lap the field, winning by 12 strokes as he had in 1997 when his dominance was announced. Instead, and to the frustration of those who believed Jack Nicklaus when he predicted 10 green jackets for Woods, he destroyed the competition by increments. In its way, this kind of play is scarier. Let the DiMarcos of the world have their fun on Thursday and Friday because, underlying each event, there is the inevitability of Woods, picking up strokes here and there until it's over. "He seems to do just what is required," said Mickelson, "and I think if I had made a run [on Sunday], he may have followed suit."

But you've got to have hope. What would be the point of tooling up Magnolia Lane year after year, packing a dreary resignation along with that new, let's say nose-high, putter. Better to believe that someone will think of something, a way to Tiger-proof the game. These are men who are familiar with desperation and, having come this far, are unyielding and resourceful in its face. Maybe some long-shot gambit, like the Super Bowl Ravens, will finally come through for a particularly daring golfer. Who knows? So, no, they will not admit to us or themselves that this really is Tiger's world and they're only in on exemptions.

Having seen what we've seen, though, we know better. At the end of the day, with the sun dropping behind the tall pines, last year's champion, Singh, slipped the green jacket over Woods's shoulders for Augusta's annual coronation. Then, heeding the calls of photographers, he did it again. The photographers wanted more, and Singh kept slipping the jacket on Woods, over and over and over, and it suddenly seemed that in some trick of time compression the future was being unspooled, however jerkily, for us. He just kept putting that jacket on, over and over and over. •

RIDING HIGH

2002 MASTERS

Augusta National debuted a course that had been "Tiger-proofed" with added trees and moved-back tees—and he won anyway.

TIGER WOODS

2002 MASTERS

Because of rain
delays Tiger
played 26 holes on
Saturday, and was
eight under
on the day.

2002 MASTERS

Tiger was tied with Retief Goosen after 54 holes, but he won comfortably by three strokes.

TIGER WOODS

At the challenging Bethpage Black, Tiger was the only golfer to finish the week below par.

2002 U.S. OPEN

2002 U.S. OPEN

The enthusiastic crowd sometimes favored his foes, but Tiger held the lead after every round.

TIGER WOODS

2002 U.S. OPEN

In the near-darkness Tiger
finished off a three-stroke win
to collect his eighth major title.

In 2004 Tiger married Elin Nordegren, who had been the nanny for Swedish golfer Jesper Parnevik. Here, in 2009, the couple watched the Orlando Magic play in the NBA Finals.

TIGER AND ELIN

Tiger waited at the 16th hole of
a rain-delayed Saturday round
in which he was locked in a tight
battle with Chris DiMarco.

2005 MASTERS

2005 MASTERS

On Saturday Tiger took
a momentary break as
he chased his fourth
green jacket.

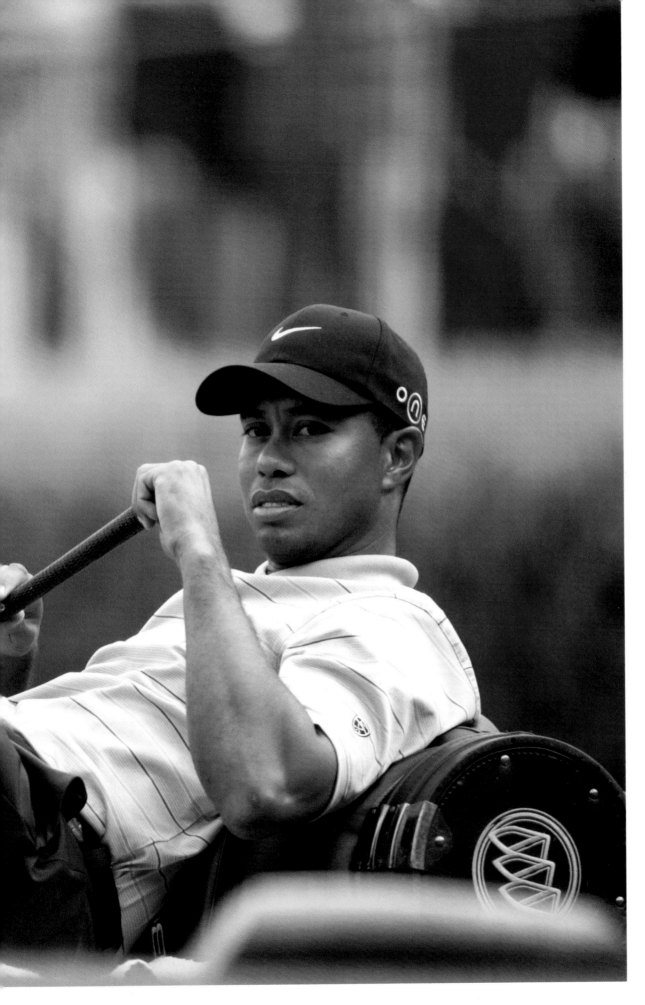

2005 MASTERS

In his critical chip-in at 16 on Sunday, Tiger watched the ball hesitate agonizingly on the lip of the cup before dropping in.

2005 MASTERS

Tiger drained an 18-foot downhill birdie putt to win a playoff with DiMarco, and his ninth major.

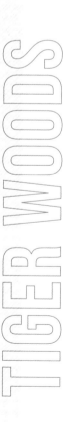

Excerpted from Sports Illustrated, April 18, 2005

The 2005 Masters

Thanks to a pitch on the 16th hole that ranks among
the most memorable shots of his career, Tiger Woods
donned a green jacket for the fourth time

by ALAN SHIPNUCK

The smile said it all, didn't it? On Sunday evening Tiger Woods stood at the back of the 18th green at Augusta National, awaiting his fate. He had just frittered away a four-stroke lead during the final round of the 69th Masters, flailing to a bogey-bogey finish that he would delicately describe later as "throwing up" on himself.

TIGER WOODS

Woods had staggered up the hill to that final green, his labored gait revealing the cumulative toll of a nerve-jangling final nine, during which he and Chris DiMarco had seemed to be playing H-O-R-S-E with their sand wedges. Now Woods had left the tournament in DiMarco's hands, in the form of a do-or-die six-foot putt to force sudden death. Moments earlier DiMarco had lipped out a chip, coming agonizingly close to a birdie that could have won the tournament—yet this pit bull in spikes refused to crack. Augusta National fairly shook when DiMarco drilled his pressure-packed par save, but Woods never flinched. Instead he flashed that big, beatific smile, a jarring sight given the enveloping tension of the moment. What was Woods thinking just then? "This is fun," he confided later.

No one in golf lives for the moment quite like Woods. With his lead slipping away, he had dealt DiMarco a body blow on the 16th hole with a seemingly impossible chip-in that instantly became one of the greatest shots in Masters history. On the first hole of sudden death, Augusta National's 18th, Woods finally landed the knockout punches. "For some reason I hit two of the best golf shots I hit all week," he said of the three-wood he busted into the narrow fairway and an eight-iron approach that covered the flag. With DiMarco in with a par, Woods faced a downhill 18-foot putt to win the Masters.

The 18th green at Augusta National is more than just a putting surface; it's the sport's grandest stage. Last year Phil Mickelson trod the boards, sinking a career-defining putt from a spot not far from where Woods's ball had come to rest. After Woods's victorious birdie putt disappeared into the cup, he loosed one of the most emotional celebrations of his career, but the overwhelming feeling was, he says, "validation."

Woods's triumph ended a much scrutinized 0-for-10 drought in the major championships. During those barren 34 months he had revamped his swing and overhauled the equipment in his bag, while also finding time to spend $1.5 million on a Caribbean wedding, donate $5 million to build an eponymous learning center in Southern California, buy a 155-foot yacht, take his first ski vacation, begin learning Swedish (the native tongue of his new bride, Elin) and buzz around South Florida looking for a new home closer to the Atlantic than his residence near Orlando. Along the way there were plenty of naysayers who whispered that the swing changes were a mistake and that maybe a domesticated Woods no longer had the focus to return to the top.

His victory last week silenced the critics and changed the sport's math. In recent months the golf world had been anticipating that this Masters would kick off a new era of parity among the so-called Big Four of Woods, Mickelson, Vijay Singh, and Ernie Els. But Woods's singular performance at Augusta reaffirmed what we've always known: There is Tiger, and then there's everybody else. You want a big four? Check out Woods's closet, because that's how many green jackets are hanging there.

Only Jack Nicklaus, with six, has more Masters titles, and with all due respect to DiMarco, last week was a reminder that Woods's only real competition is with Nicklaus's legacy of 18 major championship victories. This is Woods's

ninth full season on Tour—yes, the onetime boy wonder turns 30 on Dec. 30—and he has nine majors and counting. At the end of his ninth year as a pro, Nicklaus had eight majors.

On Sunday evening a philosophical DiMarco put into words how much this Masters has restored Woods's aura. "You know, I went out and shot 68 on Sunday, which is a very good round, and 12 under is usually good enough to win," he said. "I just was playing against Tiger Woods."

This year's model differs in significant ways from recent versions. In March 2004 Woods began working with instructor Hank Haney to build a more cohesive swing during which he maintains the same plane on the backswing and downswing. Woods's new swing began to come together in late '04, and at the season-ending Tour Championship he made another significant change: He switched to a 460cc driver with a 45-inch graphite shaft, at long last joining the space race for distance.

When Woods won the 1997 Masters by 12 strokes, he drove the ball so far with his prodigious physical gifts it seemed as if he were playing a shorter, easier course than everybody else. Wielding drivers with heads the size of toasters and composite shafts as long as fishing rods, the competition started closing the gap. Meanwhile, as late as 2003 Woods was still clinging to a retro 265cc driver with a 43.5-inch steel shaft, opting for precision over raw power. The oversized driver Woods went to six months ago helped restore some of his old distance advantage, and in January he took another leap forward by going to a hot new four-piece ball.

With his new swing and new tools Woods simply overwhelmed Augusta National last week, even though since 2001 it has been retrofitted with 305 yards of added length, expanded bunker complexes, and a forest of new trees. After opening with a hard-luck 74 that put him seven strokes behind DiMarco, Woods got back in the hunt with a second-round 66, with all but one of the holes being played on Saturday because of rain delays on Thursday and Friday. Comparing the clubs he hit to various greens during the second round with those DiMarco used highlights what a different game Woods plays compared with an average-length hitter. On the 575-yard par-5 2nd hole Woods ripped a four-iron pin-high, while DiMarco was well short of the green with a three-wood. On the 490-yard 11th hole, the portal to Amen Corner, Woods played a pitching wedge, DiMarco a three-iron. At the 500-yard par-5 15th Woods bashed a drive to the bottom of the hill and had only a nine-iron in, leading to another two-putt birdie; DiMarco missed the green with a two-iron.

When the third round commenced late Saturday afternoon, Woods and DiMarco continued to attack the softened course. Tiger bashed his way around the front nine in 31 before darkness halted play, giving him 12 birdies in 26 holes for the day and drawing him within four strokes of the precise DiMarco, who was riding a streak of 44 consecutive holes without a bogey.

Early Sunday, as Woods birdied his way through Amen Corner and DiMarco double-bogeyed the 10th hole out of a bush, Woods seized his first lead of the tournament. This was bad news for the field: Woods had never lost a major in which he was the leader after 54 holes.

In the final round Woods's advantage was still three strokes heading to the back side. DiMarco, however, wouldn't go down without a brawl. ("There's no backup in Chris," says Woods.) He rolled in a 30-footer on 11 to trim the lead to one, and then, after bogeying the dangerous 12th, stuck an approach shot to within inches on the 14th for a birdie that again drew him within one stroke.

The par-3 16th hole proved monumental. DiMarco left himself an 18-footer for birdie while Woods jacked his eight-iron long and left of the green, leaving himself little green to get to a tucked pin. His only play was to throw his pitch onto the frighteningly fast slope high above the hole and hope the ball funneled close enough to leave a realistic chance at par. As Woods's caddie, Steve Williams, said later, "We were just trying to escape with a three."

Woods picked his chip beautifully from an awkward lie against the second cut of rough, and the ball skipped onto the green, made a hard right turn, and began inching down the slope, breaking toward the cup. The ball stopped on the precipice of the hole and after a beat or two tumbled in for a birdie. Woods's play-by-play: "All of a sudden it looked pretty good. And all of a sudden it looked really good. And then it looked like how could it not go in, and how did it not go in, and all of a sudden it went in. So it was pretty sweet."

Now up by two, Woods gave a shot right back by driving into the trees on 17 and making bogey, setting the stage for the drama on the 18th hole and the ensuing playoff. After Woods had at last vanquished DiMarco, he rushed to the back of the 18th green where his mom, Tida, got the first hug, as usual, and then he planted a long, sloppy smooch on Elin. Noticeably absent among the delirium was Woods's father, Earl. A series of health problems has curtailed Earl's travel in recent years, and now he's battling cancer that began in his prostate but has spread aggressively. He rallied to make the trip to Augusta, but he was not up to navigating the crowds at the course, choosing instead to watch the tournament on TV at a rented house. In an emotional speech at the green jacket ceremony, Tiger dedicated the victory to Earl.

This palpable love between father and son brought the tournament full circle, because over the first two rounds the Nicklaus fam-

> "This is for Dad," Woods said, and now the tears were coming fast and furious, and he was gasping for breath. "Every year I've been lucky enough to win this tournament, my dad has been there to give me a hug. I can't wait to get back to the house and give him a big bear hug."

ily had provided the emotional center. Jack had said last year that 2004 might be his last Masters, but his semi-goodbye was overshadowed by Arnold Palmer's farewell. Nicklaus already was pondering whether to return this year when a family tragedy propelled him back to Augusta. On March 1 his 17-month-old grandson, Jake, drowned in a hot tub, and Jack and his grieving son Steve withdrew to the place where they are most comfortable showing their feelings, the golf course. A by-product of these 18-hole therapy sessions was that the old man felt his game coming back, and when Steve suggested that one more Masters would be a good diversion for the Nicklaus clan, Jack was happy to oblige.

Nicklaus will be at St. Andrews in July for another final hurrah on the Old Course, where he won two British Opens. Woods, too, will have good vibes when he arrives at the home of golf. At the 2000 British Open he lapped the field, winning by eight strokes, setting a tournament scoring record (19 under) and failing to hit into a single bunker over 72 holes. Woods will be the prohibitive favorite,

and he can arrive with Grand Slam dreams if he first prevails in the U.S. Open at Pinehurst No. 2, where he tied for third in 1999. With its turtleback greens, No. 2 is a shotmaker's delight that puts a premium on a creative short game. Sounds a bit like Augusta National, no?

On Sunday evening Woods deflected talk of a Grand Slam run. His mind was elsewhere. At the green jacket ceremony he told a hushed crowd, "This win is not for me, it's for my dad. It's been a difficult year, he's not doing very well. He made the trek to Augusta, but he was unable to come out and enjoy this." He stopped to gather himself.

"This is for Dad," Woods said, and now the tears were coming fast and furious, and he was gasping for breath. "Every year I've been lucky enough to win this tournament, my dad has been there to give me a hug. I can't wait to get back to the house and give him a big bear hug."

This was the logical end to a topsy-turvy day. After nearly giving away the Masters, Woods couldn't help but grin on the 72nd green. Now, in victory, he was crying when he should have been smiling again. ●

Tiger won his second British Open at the same site as his first, the Old Course at St. Andrews.

2005 BRITISH OPEN

2005 BRITISH OPEN

Tiger, who led wire-to-wire, joined Jack Nicklaus as the only golfers to have won each major twice.

TIGER WOODS

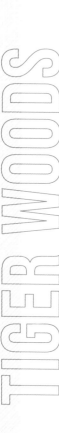

TIGER WOODS

2005 BRITISH OPEN

After his five-shot victory, Tiger referred to St. Andrews as "the home of golf."

Tiger came to Royal Liverpool after having missed the cut at the U.S. Open, the first time he had done that as a pro in a major.

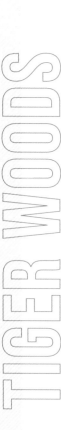

2006 BRITISH OPEN

Tiger shot an opening-round 67 that left him in a five-way tie for second.

2006 BRITISH OPEN

On Friday Tiger shot
a 65 (seven under par)
to take a one-shot
lead over Ernie Els.

2006 BRITISH OPEN

Above: On Sunday Tiger was paired
with Sergio García, one of three
golfers who trailed him by one.
Right: After winning his first major
since the death of his father,
Tiger let the tears flow.

TIGER WOODS

Excerpted from Sports Illustrated, July 21, 2006

The 2006 British Open

Tiger fought off a series of challengers to
win his 11th major, and his first since
the death of Earl Woods two months earlier

by MICHAEL BAMBERGER

A path into the heart of golf, and into the head of a golfer. Six o'clock on Saturday night, merry old England time, several hours to sunset, weirdly warm and humid. By foot, leave the village of Hoylake, a prosperous suburb 15 miles west of Liverpool's Penny Lane, past the fishmonger and the news agent and the pubs. Make the short walk to the sweet-smelling privet hedge that marks the entrance to the Royal Liverpool Golf Club. (Free admission if you're under 16.)

March over a playing field as flat as a sleeping sea, covered by a tarp of brown grass. Blow by Prince Andrew and George Clooney on your way to 17. And there, on a knobby old green first used in a British Open in 1897, take it all in: A hardworking golfer, having just missed a four-foot par putt, bent over in psychic pain. It is Tiger Woods, in transition.

At the Masters in April, playing for his dying father, Woods tried too hard and finished three shots behind the winner, Phil Mickelson. "First time I've ever seen him do that," his caddie, Steve Williams, said. Earl Woods died on May 3, and Tiger returned to golf at the U.S. Open in June, when he drove it crookedly, putted poorly, and missed the cut. He had never done that before in a major, miss the weekend in 37 starts as a pro. Last week he was back in the Kingdom—he won at St. Andrews a year ago—trying to win the 11th major of his career, at age 30. His analysis of the chessboard of a course was deeply prudent and smart, and it made you think of Ted Williams reading a pitch or Joe Montana reading his receivers or Jack Nicklaus reading the competition.

At Hoylake it became obvious that Woods is seeing a world beyond the driving range. In public comments he referred to Elin, his bride of 21 months, as "my wife."("I've never been to Italy; my wife's been there a bunch of times.") He extended his condolences to Chris DiMarco, whose mother died of a heart attack on July 4. He watched with sorrow TV clips that showed bombs and tanks and death in the Middle East. He's not living in a cocoon of golf anymore.

But the golf course is still his competitive proving ground, where for years he proved himself to his father, and now his father is gone. Last Saturday, on the 17th green, with his head over the hole, he muttered into it as if the offending jar could hear him, then left the green with his scorecard in his teeth. Tiger, you may know, is not a man prone to eccentric behavior, but with one bogey, with one misstep, he had let in the world. That's how it seemed, anyway.

By the end of Saturday's play, Sergio García of Spain, Ernie Els of South Africa, and DiMarco, a Floridian by way of Long Island, were all one shot behind Woods. Tiger 2006 is not Tiger 2000. Six years ago he drove it scary straight and very long. With the putter he holed most everything. Players wilted when he was on the top of the leaderboard. Last week at Hoylake, through two rounds and 17 holes of a third, you couldn't predict anything. Tiger's year had had no form, no rhythm, and his father was no longer available for consults. You could only wonder, as the TV ads say of Phil: What will Tiger do next? And for whom?

Usually Woods spends time in Ireland the week before the Open, for fishing and golf and cards with Marko (Mark O'Meara) and Cookie (John Cook) and the boys. This year there was no trip to Ireland, and five days be-

fore the start of the championship he began his study of the Hoylake links, which has last hosted the Open in 1967. He knew nothing about the course, but after two practice holes he had something figured out. Putting the ball in the fairway bunkers, nearly perfect rings with vertical walls made of bricks of sod, meant bogey or worse. The choice, he realized, was to play iron off the tee short of them or driver over them. But his driver, on the parched fairways, was going 350 yards or longer. "How can you control a drive that goes 375 yards?" he asked. He knew the answer. On rock-hard fairways, you can't. Working with Williams and his swing coach, Hank Haney, a game plan was hatched.

Then came the opening bell, Thursday afternoon, 1st hole, par-4, 454 yards. Crooked iron off the tee and into the rough, a two-footer for par jammed through the break, an opening bogey. There's little in tournament golf as frustrating as making a bogey when you're trying to make a safe par. For many golfers, even the best players in the world, what you do on the first hole often sets the tone for the day. At the U.S. Open, Woods opened with a bogey and made another on 2 and another on 3. His Winged Foot start had to be somewhere in his head at Royal Liverpool, right?

Wrong. Last week he buried his first-hole hiccup and opened with a 67, five under par. His eagle putt on 18 was punctuated by one of those swift Woodsian fist pumps with jaw set, lips curled, eyes narrow—expressions that make Woods look positively fierce.

His second round was an exhibition in precision golf and included the longest shot he has ever holed in competition. On the 14th, 456 yards and into a slight breeze, he hit a two-iron off the tee (bunker avoidance, bunker avoidance) and a drawing, chasing four-iron from 212 yards that kissed the metal flagstick and disappeared for an eagle. He signed for a Friday 65, a course record matched by DiMarco and, later in the day, Els, setting up this delicious third-round pairing: The front-running Tiger and Ernie in the last twosome on that weirdly warm and humid Saturday afternoon.

It brought to mind the '77 Open at Turnberry, in a rare Scottish heat wave, when Nicklaus and Tom Watson matched each other shot after amazing shot over the final 36 holes. Going into that weekend, you couldn't say who had the upper hand. (Watson won by a shot, with rounds of 65 and 65.) With the new Woods and Els still rounding into form after knee surgery last year, there was not an obvious favorite at Hoylake on Saturday, either. But the match was anticlimactic. Els, looking for his fourth major, was off line with his wedge. Tiger, with three three-putts on the back nine, the last on 17, was sloppy with the putter. Both shot 71. Three over, you could say, as the true par was more like 68. Both made birdie on the short par-5 home hole, but Saturday gave no insight into Sunday. We were watching Tiger 2006, the Tiger we don't really know. The Open was only his 10th PGA Tour event this year. In Saturday's gloaming, Woods seemed worn out, brown fescue seeds in the cuffs of his pants, sand in his ears, his eyes watery with allergies.

The toll of the majors, to head and body both, seems to be only increasing. That Tiger won four in a row, in this age of scrutiny, that Phil won two straight and nearly a third, is beyond unlikely. Mickelson revealed last month that he typically spends three days in bed after a major, and a post–U.S. Open hangover was on display last week. He prepared hard and well and early and often and finished 22nd, never remotely in it but in good cheer.

In the final round DiMarco played with Els in the penultimate twosome, and García, who tied the course record on Saturday,

played with Woods in the last. It was a zoo for both pairings, particularly for García and Woods. The fairways were clogged with Royal & Ancient officials, police officers, TV cameramen and radio reporters from several continents, marshals, scorers, rules officials, grounds crew, and fishmongers. O.K., not fishmongers; still, it was crowded. But what turned the setting into a circus was the activity behind the ropes: Cell phones with heinous ring tones going off regularly, camera phones and cheap cameras being snapped while the players were over their shots. None of the gallery's electronics are allowed, by the way, but the prohibitions were largely ignored. García's closing 73 can be attributed partly to the jangled nerves he usually shows when playing with Woods. And part, quite fairly, can be put to distraction. Woods called the Sunday situation "very, very frustrating."

But then why was Tiger's Sunday play—he shot 67—so focused, so stellar, so close to flawless? Because he is where he was. We now have a glimpse of what Tiger's coming years might look like: His past. Tiger is 11 for 11 in majors when he has had at least a share of the 54-hole lead. Talk about execution: At Hoylake he didn't hit a single fairway bunker in four rounds. He hit driver once in 72 holes, for which he shot 270, 18 under par, as if that matters to the R&A. It doesn't. Next month—at the PGA Championship at Medinah, where he held off García in '99—we'll find out whether Tiger can keep the driver in play.

But links golf has always been about iron play—and wind. By Tiger's count, he missed only three iron shots all week. O.K., the wind was very meager, not a totally thorough test. Still, in an era when the long iron is practically dead, Woods showed his long-iron play is alive and well. He controlled his distances by controlling the trajectory. The excellence of his strikes was announced by the clouds of dirt and grass kicked up by his clubhead.

Will he get to 19 professional majors, one past Nicklaus's record total and Woods's holy grail? It'll be hard. One a year from 2007 through 2014, when he'll be 38, would do it, but that's a huge task. Yes, golfers these days are competitive beyond 40. Tom Watson and Fred Funk, combined age 106, made the cut last week. But Woods has been playing on the big stage for 15 years already. For any pro to play at the top of his game for a decade is substantial. With all that he has accomplished, it's daunting to think he has nearly a decade more to go (at one a year).

But we know more about him now, this golfer and man in transition, than we did when he stood on the 17th green on Saturday, when he could have gone either way in the championship's final 19 holes. We know now that Tiger Woods, playing for his mother and his wife and himself and his legacy and in his father's memory, is capable not only of stunning golf, but also of summoning his talent when he most wants it. It didn't happen at Augusta, it didn't happen at Winged Foot, but it happened at Royal Liverpool, and one for three in golf is outstanding. We know that he's evolving as a man in appealing ways.

(Nicklaus did the same in his 30s.) We know now that his father's death did not rob him of emotion. If anything, it did the opposite.

Tiger's long, sobbing post victory hug with Williams brought to mind another famous golf embrace. Not the hug Tiger shared with his father in '97, when he won the Masters for the first time, at age 21, by 12 shots. That was all about, "We did it." That was all about, "We showed 'em." The hug on Sunday brought to mind a scene at Augusta in '95, when the winner, Ben Crenshaw, was comforted by his caddie, Carl Jackson, days after Gentle Ben had buried his teacher and surrogate father, Harvey Penick. The SI cover line was, ONCE MORE, WITH FEELING. Still works.

Tiger was asked about the hug, of course. He said, "It just came pouring out of me, all the things my dad meant to me, and the game of golf. I just wish he could have seen it one more time." He said, "I've never done that before. You know me."

Actually, we don't. But we know him better than we did last week. You can see a trip to Italy coming, with the missus, drinking Chianti out of the claret jug, the clubs stashed in a Florida closet. One more major first, though. ●

> **"**
>
> **Tiger was asked about the hug, of course. He said, "It just came pouring out of me, all the things my dad meant to me, and the game of golf. I just wish he could have seen it one more time."**

2006 PGA CHAMPIONSHIP

2006 PGA

Tiger teed off at 18
on Sunday, on his way
to a five-shot win
over Shaun Micheel.

2006 PGA

Above: Woods and Phil Mickelson were paired in the early rounds (Mickelson would tie for 16th). Right: On Sunday Woods enjoyed what he afterward called "the ultimate rush" of closing in on a major.

Tiger collected his seventh consecutive stroke-play win at the Buick Invitational at Torrey Pines in January 2007. The streak, which dated back to the 2006 British Open, is the longest of his career.

SEVEN IN A ROW

In pursuit of his second consecutive PGA Championship, Tiger teed off at the ninth hole of the Southern Hills Country Club in Tulsa.

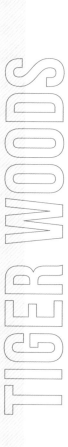

2007 PGA

The average
temperature in
Tulsa for the week
was 101 degrees,
with the heat
index reaching 110.

2007 PGA

Woods, after shooting
a 63 in the second
round, a career low for
a major, followed it with
rounds of 69 on both
Saturday and Sunday
for a two-shot win over
Woody Austin.

TIGER WOODS

2007 PGA

Tiger's 13th major
win tied him on
the career list
with Bobby Jones.

Woods parred the 17th hole on Sunday, meaning he needed a birdie on 18 to force a playoff with Rocco Mediate.

TIGER WOODS

2008 US OPEN

Tiger played with
stress fractures in
his tibia and knee;
after this tournament
he would not compete
again until March 2009.

TIGER WOODS

2008 U.S. OPEN

Tiger dropped
in disappointment
during Monday's
playoff after a
long birdie putt
came up short.

TIGER WOODS

2008 U.S. OPEN

Tiger was so emotional about
his Sunday birdie at 18 that
he had both fists pumping.

Excerpted from SPORTS ILLUSTRATED, June 23, 2008

TIGER WOODS

The 2008 U.S. Open

To win his 14th major championship, a hobbled
Tiger Woods needed to endure an extra round on Monday
while gutting his way through agonizing pain

by ALAN SHIPNUCK

Tiger Woods has defined his career in terms of major championship victories, and in turn they have defined him. Some wins have been monuments to his power, as when he obliterated the old Augusta National in 1997, and others have been tributes to his precision, such as the 2000 British Open, when he navigated the heaving earth of the Old Course without hitting into a single bunker.

Woods has separated himself with clutch putting, as at the '06 PGA Championship when he canned a pair of 40-footers early in the final round, and he has dazzled as a tactician, taking apart Southern Hills one little swing at a time at the '07 PGA.

Woods's unique skill set was on display again at last week's U.S. Open, but this victory was more visceral. It was all heart.

Playing for the first time since arthroscopic knee surgery two months ago, Woods was sore, stiff, and rusty when he arrived at Torrey Pines Golf Course in La Jolla, Calif., a 7,643-yard brute that was easily the longest track

in major championship history. Over four riveting rounds and a taxing 19-hole Monday playoff, Woods didn't play the golf course so much as brawl with it, his left leg occasionally buckling mid-swing, his face often twisted into a mask of pain, audible grunts and groans escaping after so many shots. Yet this son of a Green Beret simply soldiered on. Woods snatched this Open with typically heroic flourishes, but his 14th major championship triumph was mostly about a palpable refusal to give in—to the pain, to an exacting course, and to anyone trying to take a trophy that Woods considered to be rightfully his.

After four days of scrappy golf Woods came to the par-5 72nd hole on Sunday trailing Rocco Mediate by a stroke. A bad drive into a fairway bunker and a sloppy layup left him in the tangly right rough, 101 yards from a dangerous pin cut hard against a green-front pond. Woods muscled a wedge shot to within 12 feet, and our national championship was suddenly distilled into a moment thrilling in its simplicity: Make the putt or go home. One of Earl Woods's most famous quotes was actually a whisper into his son's ear at a critical juncture of a long-ago U.S. Amateur: "Let the legend grow." It grows, still. Woods buried the putt, setting up the 18-hole playoff with Mediate, a likable 45-year-old veteran with a bad back and loose lips and not the foggiest idea of what he had gotten himself into.

On Monday, Mediate battled bravely and actually outplayed Woods tee-to-green but he could not match his opponent's resourcefulness. Mediate, who rallied from a three-shot deficit with eight holes left, was at even par and one stroke ahead playing the 18th hole but for the second straight day could only make a disappointing par. When Woods summoned a textbook two-putt birdie the two moved on to sudden death. On the first extra hole Woods played two flawless shots and Mediate finally cracked, going from a fairway bunker to greenside rough en route to a fatal bogey.

For Woods the victory was deeply satisfying on any number of levels. This is his third U.S. Open championship but first in six years, and in the annals of the tournament he now trails only four-time winners Willie Anderson, Bobby Jones, Ben Hogan, and Jack Nicklaus. With his 14 career majors Woods has crept ever closer to Nicklaus's epic total of 18, and it is mind-boggling to think that at 32 he is potentially one great calendar year away from attaining the unattainable.

Woods will always be most closely identified with the Masters because of the sociopolitical overtones of his breakthrough victory in 1997 and because the exquisitely manicured course allows him to display both his creativity and his power. The U.S. Open, however, is more reflective of what Woods is all

"

Over four riveting rounds and a taxing 19-hole Monday playoff, Woods didn't play the golf course so much as brawl with it, his left leg occasionally buckling mid-swing, his face often twisted into a mask of pain, audible grunts and groans escaping after so many shots. Yet this son of a Green Beret simply soldiered on.

Tiger made the playoff when his 12-footer on 18 lipped the cup and dropped.

about. It's a grinder's tournament, a nonstop stress fest that pushes players to the breaking point, and sometimes beyond. Woods revels in the punishment doled out by the Open, and last week he performed a kind of golfing rope-a-dope in which he was willing to absorb the shooting pain in his knee and the sting of his four double bogeys because he knew the ensuing triumph would be that much sweeter.

"It was a great battle," Woods said afterward. He was speaking of Mediate in particular, but he could have meant so much more. Asked how this one rates among all of his majors, Woods said, "I think this one is the best, just because of all the things I had to deal with."

Like Ali and Jordan, Woods doesn't simply want to win—he wants to beat you. It's personal with him, and to that point the USGA, as part of a plan to have the top players in the World Ranking on the course at the same time, helped spur Woods by matching him with Phil Mickelson and world No. 3 Adam Scott over the first two rounds, a blockbuster threesome that left everybody else in the field playing to a sound track of crickets and cheering family members. Woods needed the adrenaline provided by playing with Mickelson to make him whole because on April 17, two days after the Masters concluded, he had surgery on his left knee to repair cartilage damage (the third operation on the same knee since 1994). In the run-up to the Open, Woods was reduced mostly to chipping and putting, and during his practice rounds at Torrey he never played more than nine holes. Though he still had a noticeable limp, Woods tried to downplay his condition on the eve of the tournament, saying, "I'm good to go. I plan on being competitive. Come game time I'll be ready."

It's easy to forget, given his superstar sheen, that Woods grew up as a golf nerd. Vanity is part of what has driven him to build his body to superhero dimensions; knowing that the general public largely considers golfers to be weenies, Woods repeatedly downplayed how much his knee was bothering him. His swing coach, Hank Haney, provided a more honest assessment: "He's hurting more than anybody knows."

With all the attention trained on the Tiger and Phil show, almost no one noticed Mediate's opening rounds of 69–71. Mediate was tied with Woods and by his own admission just happy to be there. A year and a half ago he was working as a commentator for the Golf Channel as back ailments had put his playing career on hold, an all-too-familiar setback as the purity of Mediate's ball striking is matched only by the brittleness of his body. At the 2006 Masters he was tied for the lead playing the 9th hole on Sunday when his back went out, and he hobbled his way to a 10 on the par-3 12th hole. The soothing hands of a new physical therapist have helped Mediate revive his career, but he punched his ticket to Torrey only by surviving an 11-man playoff (for seven spots) in Open qualifying. At 157th in the World Ranking, Mediate knew he was out of his depth heading into the weekend. "It's going to be nerve-racking and insane the next few days," he said.

Yet on Saturday it was Woods who looked jittery as he played the first 12 holes in three over par. His round, and the tournament, turned on the 13th, though it didn't begin auspiciously, as he blew his drive miles right of the fairway. Because of the ball's close proximity to a concession stand, Woods received a free drop, and he caught a good lie in an area of rough that had been trampled by the gallery. He then ripped a five-iron to the back of the green, leaving himself a breaking 65-foot downhill putt. Two thirds of the way there the eagle putt was as good as in, and when the ball disappeared Woods uncorked one of his lustiest celebrations in recent memory.

The pyrotechnics were just beginning. On the par-4 17th his third shot from the greenside rough came out hot, took one big hop, hit a couple of feet up the flagstick, and dropped in the hole. It was equal parts good aim and good luck, and Woods knew it judging by his sheepish smile. He kept the momentum going on 18 with two perfect shots, leaving himself 30 feet for another eagle.

On a day when he was fighting his swing and his knee, Woods had stolen a round of 70 that could have—should have—been a half-dozen strokes higher.

With a much more mundane third round of 72, Mediate was two strokes off Woods's lead and a shot back of England's Lee Westwood, who was bidding to become the first European to win the Open since Tony Jacklin in 1970. History was not on the side of the pursuers, as Woods was 13 for 13 in converting 54-hole leads into victory at the majors.

Yet Woods gave everybody hope on Sunday by making a mess of the 1st hole again, hitting a smother-hook off the tee and then doinking trees on his next two swings on his way to a double bogey. When Woods three-putted the 2nd hole he was suddenly two back of Mediate. Tiger steadied himself in the middle part of his round, and a pinpoint three-iron set up a birdie on the par-3 11th that put him back in the lead. But he gave it up twice with bogeys at 13 and 15.

Woods might never have had a shot at redemption had Mediate made a birdie on the 18th, but a cautious wedge doomed Rocco to a par. Westwood had a 20-footer for birdie to join the playoff, but the putt was timid. In the end only Woods could summon the necessary final-hole magic.

On Sunday, Woods sat for a press conference that featured the inevitable Father's Day question, a softball designed to elicit a gooey response about his daughter, Sam, who was born the day after last year's Open. Unabashed sentiment has defined many of Woods's majors, from the joyous hug with his dad behind the 18th green at the 1997 Masters to the torrent of tears at the 2006 British Open, a couple of months after Earl's death. Now Woods was on the verge of his bravest victory yet, a performance that laid bare his unbreakable will and phenomenal focus. So, he was asked, "Years from now when your daughter is old enough to understand, what do you want her to know about what you did this week, considering the knee?"

He could have answered in so many ways, but Woods offered only four words that perfectly captured who he is: "I got a W." ●

FALL AND RISE

Tiger delivered a 13½-minute statement in February 2010 to a small audience that included his mother (in black).

THE APOLOGY

Excerpted from SPORTS ILLUSTRATED, March 1, 2010

Shrinking Before Us

His veneer of perfection shattered by revelations of personal scandal, Tiger Woods appeared as a diminished man when he made a long-awaited public apology

by ALAN SHIPNUCK

The TV cameras are supposed to add 10 pounds, but they have long made Tiger Woods larger than life. In person his dimensions can seem almost boyish—he has a wasp waist and delicate wrists. But throughout Woods's already legendary playing career, the oversized flat screens that fill up America's living rooms could scarcely contain his overwhelming physical presence.

On the golf course he strutted in the cocksure manner of a toreador. Opponents shrank in Woods's presence, and golf courses often were reduced to pitch-and-putts.

That's what made Woods's public apology so jarring, in the wake of a series of revelations about marital infidelities, and following his emergence from a 45-day treatment program. It wasn't so much what he said, it was how diminished he looked, obscured by a podium and swallowed up by a too-big blazer that recalled a coat borrowed by a teenager who had been forced to put on a jacket at a fancy restaurant.

But what this scandal has belatedly taught us is that despite all the trappings of an adult life, Tiger had never really grown up. His wife, Elin, is a proud and independent woman who refused to be a prop in his stage-managed apology. So it was left to Woods's mother, Tida, to be the star of Friday's telecast. She was seated prominently in the front row, her face twisted into a mask of pain and worry. Forget the millions of viewers at home—is there anything more mortifying for a grown man than having to talk about your sex life in front of your mom? No wonder Woods seemed so awkward reading his prepared remarks.

During his 13½-minute address Woods repeatedly apologized for his myriad mistakes, but he didn't exactly take ownership of them. "I felt that I had worked hard my entire life and deserved to enjoy all the temptations around me," he said. "I felt I was entitled. Thanks to money and fame, I didn't have to go far to find them."

In the run-up to Woods's first public appearance in nearly three months, his management company, IMG, was criticized for the heavy-handed control it exerted on the proceedings. It's clear now that Woods needed the coddling; he seemed so shaky emotionally it's doubtful he could have withstood any exposure to an inquisitive press corps. The instinct to shelter and protect runs deep in his inner circle. After Woods's remarks, his caddie, Steve Williams, told Australia's *Sun-Herald* newspaper, "Nothing changes."

Actually, everything has changed. Woods said he doesn't know when he will return to golf, and judging by his fragility, it won't be any time soon. At some point he will reclaim his destiny as a golfer, but it is now an open question whether he will be the same player he was. Part of what made Woods such a relentless achiever was his selfishness. He gave nothing beyond his performance. He played the gentleman's game in a controlled rage, hocking loogies, chucking clubs, and dropping f-bombs. If you didn't like it, too bad. All his recent soul-searching, though, has convinced Woods that he is not exempt from golf's code of conduct. "When I do return, I need to make my behavior more respectful of the game," he said. Easier said than done, perhaps: Tiger is not Arnie, who could play with controlled fury, then throttle back once the final putt had dropped.

When Woods does return, it will be to his new tabloid reality. Woods practically snarled one line in addressing the media: "Whatever my wrongdoings, for the sake of my family, please leave my wife and kids alone." He does not seem to grasp that his misadventurous

lifestyle invited the paparazzi's lens. Before his single-car accident at 2:30 a.m. on Black Friday that opened the door to all these revelations, he was considered so dull that the tabloids and much of the mainstream media had no use for him. (Publicly, anyway; Woods cooperated on a story with *Men's Fitness* magazine after its parent publishing company allegedly agreed not to reveal personal details.) Going forward, Woods and his family will face an unrelenting glare.

During his career Woods has let the public into his heart only twice: The hug with his father, Earl, that punctuated Tiger's 12-stroke victory at the 1997 Masters; and the teary embrace with Elin behind the final green at the 2006 British Open, Tiger's first win following Earl's death. At the conclusion of his prepared remarks, Woods haltingly walked to his mother for a long, sorrowful embrace. These three hugs neatly encapsulate his wrenching journey from young master to grown man to little boy lost. ●

Tiger walked off after making his first public appearance in three months.

Tiger signed autographs at the 2012 Arnold Palmer Invitational, where he would win for the first time since 2009.

2012 ARNOLD PALMER INVITATIONAL

2012 ARNOLD PALMER INVITATIONAL

At the 18th Tiger completed his seventh Tour win at Bay Hill; he would win there again in 2013 to reclaim golf's No. 1 ranking.

Excerpted from Sports Illustrated, April 8, 2013

The Road Back

Three years after his world blew up,
Tiger Woods was winning again, and finding
joy in his reconfigured life

by MICHAEL ROSENBERG

In April 2010, in his first tournament since the world started laughing at him, Tiger Woods sprayed shots all over Augusta National. He did finish fourth at the Masters, a testament to his talent, will, and ability to scramble. But before his private plane left Augusta, he told his longtime friend John Cook that he wasn't fooled.

"He says, 'I'm so confused right now, I don't know what to do,'" Cook recalls. "'I don't know what my golf swing is supposed to do.'"

When Woods got home to Orlando, he met Cook at their home club, Isleworth. Cook had previously sensed tension in Woods's relationship with his swing instructor, Hank Haney, but had kept quiet. At Isleworth, Cook asked Woods pointed questions: Do you like your direction? Are you happy with Hank? In the past Woods had betrayed nothing, merely promising to grind his way back to dominance. This time, Cook says, "He was beyond spinning it with, 'I really need to get to work.' You could really tell he felt lost."

In a career of firsts, this was another: Tiger Woods, lost on a golf course. Haney quit after that Masters. (Friends suspect Woods would have fired him anyway.) At times during that 2010 season, Woods looked like something he had never been: A hacker. To this day Woods—publicly at least—blames injuries, and the four surgeries to his left knee have had a cumulative effect. But health was hardly his only problem.

You, of course, are familiar with the backstory. On Thanksgiving weekend of 2009, Woods had crashed his Cadillac SUV into a fire hydrant outside his house, throwing his life into turmoil. One tabloid report that he had been unfaithful to his wife, Elin, metastasized into dozens more. Woods became the star of a daily reality show that he couldn't cancel.

For his whole career, despite being the most scrutinized golfer in history, Woods had kept his golf game in a cocoon. He played entire rounds without directly acknowledging a single fan. Interviews were rare (and still are; Woods declined to talk to Sports Illustrated for this piece).

His father, Earl, whom Tiger adored, was a philanderer, and Cook says Tiger had vowed he would not make the same mistake. Now he had, and everybody knew it. Even casual fans were disgusted.

The pain was self-inflicted, and it was intense. The cocoon had vanished. Woods was flailing in golf and life. The world was watching. And Woods, who always seemed oblivious to the masses, was watching the world watch him. "He'd say, 'Did you see that TMZ thing?'" Cook recalls. "'I'm not [up] on TMZ, so I don't really care. He would pay attention to that. And something was on every day."

Woods had displayed a temper on the course for most of his career, but now the outbursts were louder and affected his play. His interactions with the media, which had been cool but civil, became contentious. Initially there were concerns in Tiger's inner circle that the galleries would razz him mercilessly, but that didn't happen. The misery came from within.

"It's like mixing three or four colors of paint," says former PGA Tour player Notah Begay, one of Woods's best friends since childhood. "Once it's done, you can't unmix it. Once you have all these components in play—the media, the scandal, the personal history, the performance—it's like this chaos. And it's hard to make sense of that in front of everybody.

"I'm not saying one person's turmoil is any more or less important than anybody else's, but having to experience that in front of the world—having everybody at the grocery market, the gas station, the gym knowing exactly what you did, who you did it with, and how it's adversely impacted [your] life—multiplies the impact it has on [your] emotional stability and psyche. It was evident in his play. He was not very focused."

Woods had long leaned on his interactions with famous men, iconic men, from Michael Jordan to Muhammad Ali to Nelson Mandela, to learn how to handle global celebrity. But in 2010 he was stuck.

"I know him as well as anybody," Begay says, "and I had no advice."

Woods had endured minislumps before. But those struggles had merely brought him closer to the field; they had not made him part of it. At age five he was so good that the best 15-year-old golfers in Southern California viewed him as a peer. They ate lunch with him, joked with him, and competed against him. Years later this would be spun as part of Earl Woods's grand plan, but Tiger's first coach, Rudy Duran, says it wasn't planned at all. "I provided the same outlet to hundreds of other kids," Duran says. "Earl was way less pushy, way less trying to groom a touring pro than most of these parents."

The father was not obsessed. The child was. Tiger played golf to the point of exhaustion, then fell asleep in the car on the way home. His parents had to push him away from the course, toward school.

Earl was so amazed that he kept raising expectations in public. He'd show up at a junior tournament and casually announce that his son would win. By the time Tiger turned pro, in the summer of 1996, Earl famously told SI, "I was personally selected by God himself...to nurture this young man.... Tiger will do more than any other man in history to change the course of humanity."

Really?

"Earl was an idiot," says John Anselmo, Tiger's coach from ages 10 to 18, with a laugh that lets you know he is talking about a friend. "I loved him, but he was an idiot. He was bragging about his son like crazy, and he was overdoing it."

Tiger wasn't trying to change the course of humanity. Given the choice between golf and anything else, Tiger chose golf. Anselmo says that even when pretty girls walked past the driving range, the young Tiger barely noticed.

It was commonly accepted that Tiger was hunting Jack Nicklaus's record of 18 majors. Friends say that isn't quite true. Sure, he had a poster of Nicklaus in his childhood bedroom. But many kids own posters of their heroes. Trip Kuehne, who competed against Tiger as an amateur and became a good friend, says the record never came up between them.

Begay, however, says Woods has a number in mind now. But it isn't 18. "He is focused on 20," Begay says. "That may be a little hard to believe, considering what's transpired in the last three years, but that's where his focus is. He thinks he is capable of winning 20 majors."

Why 20? Because that is what Tiger thinks he can accomplish. And if he reaches 20, he will hunt for 21; if he remains stuck on 14, he'll keep hunting for 15. He is not driven by the external approval that would come with passing Nicklaus. More than winning the Masters, he wants to master the game.

"It's a huge distinction," says Conrad Ray, Woods's college teammate and now the Stanford coach. "He is happy he has all those trophies on the wall, but to me it's the game within the game that really drives him."

As a teenager Woods would hit a perfect shot on the range, then immediately try something else. After winning the 1997 Masters by 12 strokes, he decided to change his swing because he thought he could improve. After winning four straight majors with his new swing in 2000–01, he rebuilt it again.

Since 2010 he has undergone the most dramatic changes of all. Woods has revamped his swing yet again; been divorced; hired a new instructor; switched caddies; changed putters; recovered from knee and Achilles-tendon injuries; moved from inland Orlando to the coastal Florida town of Jupiter, where he and Elin share custody of their five-year-old daughter, Sam, and four-year-old son, Charlie; switched home courses; started dating Olympic skier Lindsey Vonn; and returned to No. 1 in the World Ranking.

Woods has won six of his last 20 official events and, for the first time in five years, he is the favorite in the Masters, which begins on April 11. The Nicklaus comparisons are heating up again, but you rarely hear this one: Nicklaus did not play golf seriously until he was 10 years old. Woods was a prodigy before he turned three. Woods cannot remember a single day in his life that was not colored, in some way, by his obsession with golf. Almost all of his relationships were formed in the shadow of his greatness.

Over lunch at the Doral Golf Resort near Miami in mid-March, Begay is asked: When Woods's infidelities became public, what was his biggest worry? Begay thinks for a moment.

"I think his biggest concern at that point was just: Who, of his closest friends, might judge him?" Begay says. "He knew the media was going to be hard on him—sports media, the mainstream media, and tabloid media. I think he was concerned about what his friends thought." Woods apologized to them individually.

This was an adjustment for him. Woods had never had to ingratiate himself with others. His talent drew people to him.

Former Tour pro Casey Martin explains. Martin can't walk long distances because of a rare circulatory disorder in his right leg, and in the 1990s he sued the PGA Tour for the right to use a cart in competition. Nicklaus

> **The pain was self-inflicted, and it was intense. The cocoon had vanished. Woods was flailing in golf and life. The world was watching. And Woods, who always seemed oblivious to the masses, was watching the world watch him.**

and Arnold Palmer spoke against his position, arguing that walking was an integral part of the game.

Woods, Martin's old Stanford teammate and friend, was in a better position to help him than anybody else. But, Martin says, "I wouldn't say he was overly supportive. He made a few comments, but I think he wanted to stay out of it." The case went all the way to the U.S. Supreme Court, which ruled in Martin's favor. Like many college friends, Woods and Martin lost touch for several years. But Martin's feelings never changed.

"I pull for Tiger like you can't believe," says Martin, who coaches the Oregon men's team. "I've never pulled for a guy like [I do for] Tiger. I don't know what that comes from. When you see somebody who is so different and so special, you're mesmerized. I always find myself going, Why do I pull for this guy so much? When he was struggling, gosh, it hurt me. I'm like, Come on! I want him to break every record. I can't help it."

That social equation—when Tiger did not put in the effort to please others, his talent made up the difference—played out in his favor a thousand times in a hundred ways.

Duran, his first coach, worked with him from ages four to 10 without getting paid. ("I can't charge for having fun," Duran says. "It didn't feel right, so I didn't.") Anselmo did not get paid either, though Woods did pay some of his medical bills after turning pro.

Haney wrote in his 2012 book, *The Big Miss*, that Woods paid him only $50,000 per year, plus a $25,000 bonus when Woods won a major. Haney also wrote that Woods apparently had no interest in being his friend, no matter what he did. Yet Haney tells SI, "Honestly, I would pay him for that job. He knows that."

Spectators were on the same side of that social equation. Woods went entire rounds without making eye contact with them. He seemed inhumanly unflappable, an effect enhanced by his Nike golf outfits. They breathe where he sweats, so you don't see moisture on his shirt, and he doesn't have to pull at his sleeves or hike up his trousers, because they fit perfectly.

Shortly after turning pro in 1996, Woods signed a two-book deal with Warner Books. He worked on every detail of his first book, *How I Play Golf*, and it became a runaway best seller. His second book was supposed to be an autobiography. Woods never wrote it.

For years, sportswriters complained that Woods never said anything interesting. But they praised him relentlessly. "From 1997 to 2005, I'll bet you [there were] 200 times a media person said to me: 'I'm doing a piece on Tiger Woods. Can you give me some good adjectives?'" says PGA Tour commissioner Tim Finchem. "They were just trying to one-up each other—how gushy they could be over Tiger Woods."

When Woods crashed his Cadillac, the gushing stopped. The public soon hop-scotched to the next celebrity scandal, but Woods struggled to move on. As he did so, he had to choose pieces of his old life to carry into his new one.

In August 2010, the same month his divorce became final, Woods asked fellow pro Sean O'Hair for the phone number of O'Hair's old coach Sean Foley. They worked together for several sessions. At the end of September, after seven straight finishes outside the top 10, Woods hired Foley, officially forming one of the most misunderstood relationships in sports.

Foley sounds more like a science professor than somebody teaching a sport. He talks about swing dynamics, as in, "A dynamic is: How do I create energy through my pelvis? How do I use the ground to create energy? A dynamic is: If the face is pointed two degrees right, and the movement of the sweet spot through the golf ball is four degrees right, with a seven-iron you're going to hit a ball that's going to start right and curve back."

Foley hears people say the golf swing should be simple and says, incredulously, "Keep it simple? How? You're talking about energy systems, velocities and linear speeds.... There is nothing simple about it."

Partly because of the science talk, analysts have accused Foley of trying to turn Woods into a robot. The truth is, of Woods's three professional coaches—Butch Harmon, Haney, and Foley—Foley is the most inclined to give Woods space.

Foley sees Woods on the driving range before a round, says, "Hey, bro," and moves on. He senses that Woods wants his space. Foley does not give Woods a pre-shot routine, tell him what clubs to swing in warmups, or discuss equipment. He rarely talks to Woods about putting.

Foley eats lunch with Woods regularly when they work together but estimates they have eaten dinner together twice. He has been to Woods's new mansion in Jupiter but not often. He would rather save time and meet at Woods's new home course, Medalist Golf Club. It's their office. After tournament rounds, whether Woods shoots 65 or 75, their routine is the same.

"We don't go back and work on the things that didn't work that day," Foley says. "We just keep in the system, in the system, in the system, until that is a highly insulated neural circuit, and in time of pressure or distress or whatever, that's what the brain allocates, rather than an old one or an in-between one. It's not about fixes at all."

Translated into English: He wants Woods's swing to hold up under pressure. He gives detailed answers to Woods's questions but doesn't micromanage his swing thoughts.

Cook says that Haney would send Woods "to the first tee with a scroll of stuff [to remember]. It was like he had that quarterback playlist on his arm. I like Hank, and I've known him a long time. [But] the time I spent with them together...I'm listening and going, Wow, that sounds really complicated to me. I didn't think they needed to be doing that."

Haney says he didn't worry about over-loading Woods, because "he always told me, I'll process it. I'll pare it down. Don't hold back." And Haney frequently points out that

Woods won 31 of 91 events when they worked together, and six majors in six years. For any player in history that is extraordinary. But how do you compare the incomparable? How can anybody know what Woods would have done from ages 28 to 34 with another instructor?

Before his divorce Woods had always sought the advice of older, wiser men—not just Anselmo, Harmon, and Haney but also Mark O'Meara and Cook, Isleworth neighbors who are a generation older. Foley is a peer who doesn't see Woods as a protégé.

Ten months after hiring Foley, Woods made another bold move: He fired his long-time caddie, the brash Kiwi Steve Williams. Williams was both adviser and protector—barking at photographers, glaring at spectators, publicly feuding with Phil Mickelson. Williams and Woods were groomsmen at each other's weddings.

Woods never explained the firing publicly. But his hiring of caddie Joe LaCava in September 2011 is telling. LaCava's skills are highly respected—he was on Fred Couples's bag for years and Dustin Johnson's as well—but he is also incorrigibly easygoing. Woods signaled that he no longer wanted his caddie to act like a bodyguard.

Haney seemed to covet Woods's friendship. Williams prized it. LaCava says he and Foley are "not looking for a friendship. Yet he makes you feel like he's your best buddy."

LaCava stayed at Woods's house for the Honda Classic, and when Woods triumphed at Torrey Pines, he told LaCava, "We won this f------ tournament!" LaCava thought, We didn't win anything.

In the past Woods snapped at caddies and coaches. LaCava says Woods has not blamed him for a bad club choice or read on the green.

Woods now had a coach he trusted, a caddie who simply caddied, and a swing that reduced stress on his left knee. His game and his life were coming back. On Sept. 30, 2011—six

months after joining Medalist and almost exactly a year after he hired Foley—Woods made five straight birdies on Medalist's back nine en route to a course-record 62.

In November 2011, Woods flew to Australia for the Australian Open and the Presidents Cup. He seemed more at ease than he had been in years. He bantered with people he did not know very well and was in no rush to leave the room.

"Everybody felt really comfortable around him," Cook says. "It hasn't always been that way in these events."

Woods's friend Steve Stricker says, "I think he learned a lot from a couple of years ago: Be more cordial to everybody, respect other people. He is happier with himself. You can see it. Just the way he is treating people is better. It looks like he is working hard at it."

In March 2012, Woods won his first official tournament since the tabloid storm. Now he looks like the best player in the world.

"If Tiger gets to 19 majors, they're going to write amazing articles about me," Foley says. "The fact of the matter is, it has nothing to do with me. I don't have to go out on the course and deal with fear and gallery noise and slow play and figure out where the wind is and what the divot's telling me. I don't have to deal with any of that."

Foley doesn't even watch a lot of it. As Woods played his opening round at Doral last month, Foley walked the course following another of his players, Justin Rose. A spectator recognized Foley as Woods's coach and told him, "I think you're doing a great job."

"Thanks, man," Foley said.

"It's really cool to watch," the fan continued.

"Thanks, man."

After the spectator walked away, Foley said, "That is nice of him to say that, but I don't care—just like when the guy goes, 'I think you're s---. I think you're ruining the game.'"

The Medalist Golf Club, in Hobe Sound,

Fla., is where worldwide fame meets Florida wildlife. In any given round you might encounter alligators, PGA Tour stars Dustin Johnson and Rickie Fowler, rattlesnakes, British Open champions Ian Baker-Finch and Mark Calcavecchia, pumas, Dan Marino, and No. 1–ranked LPGA player Stacy Lewis, more rattlesnakes, or Tiger Woods, who joined in March 2011.

Look: There is three-time major champion Nick Price having a drink in the clubhouse. And yes, that man wearing a striped Masters shirt in the parking lot really is legendary quarterback Peyton Manning, who just played 18 holes as a guest. At the Medalist's member-guest tournament this month, Woods partnered with broadcaster Ahmad Rashad, while fellow member Michael Jordan teamed with guest Keegan Bradley.

Medalist is a golfer's golf club. It's open for dinner only one night a week: Wednesday, when there is a buffet. There are no houses on the course. (A few houses have a view of the 3rd hole, but they are not affiliated with Medalist.) The clubhouse is nice but not gaudy. Cart paths are sand.

"There are no rules," club president De Mudd says. There are also no tee times. The best players in the world play in shorts, with shirts untucked. They can play alone or in fivesomes; play music from their carts, as long as nobody complains; play all 18 or hit six tee shots on one hole, as long as nobody has to wait behind them.

In the inverted reality of Woods's life—his house is visible from the water but not the street, and he released photos of himself with Vonn so the media would leave them alone—he needs a place as exclusive as Medalist to feel most like a commoner.

He calls staffers by their first names and chats with them before heading to the 1st tee. He says hello at the halfway house and goes on his way, like any other member instead of one of the most famous athletes in the world.

He enjoys the kind of golf test he has loved since childhood: A firm and fast course where the wind kicks up and Woods has to be creative to score well. A few Sundays ago he invited Rory McIlroy over for a 36-hole duel—Woods won the first 18, McIlroy the second—and Bubba Watson says they often play matches.

Woods plays as many as 45 holes in a day, and when he isn't at Medalist he practices at the short-game facility at his house. The kid who used to pound balls into a net in his parents' garage now hits full nine-irons in his backyard along Jupiter Sound.

But he does not cling to that cocoon the way he did. For years, when Woods played the annual Tour stop at Torrey Pines in San Diego, he would curtly say hello when the starter gave him his scorecard. Business. Fans standing a few feet away had no idea that Woods had known the starter, Tony Perez, for most of his life. Tony's son, PGA Tour player Pat Perez, competed against Woods as a child and remains a friend. On Sunday of this year's tournament, Woods took his card, smiled, and hugged Tony.

"He just wrapped his arms around me and wouldn't let go," Perez says. "I told him, 'Welcome back.'"

In the spring of 2012, after qualifying for the U.S. Open at Olympic in San Francisco, Casey Martin was pleasantly surprised to see this tweet from @TigerWoods: "Simply incredible. Ability, attitude and guts. See you at Olympic Casey."

Woods added a link to a story about Martin. The college friends had not talked in years, but they played a practice round together at Olympic. After all those years of rooting for Woods, Martin knew that Woods was rooting for him too.

"Everything is so stable now," Begay says. "Tiger and Elin are on better terms, for the

> **The Nicklaus comparisons are heating up again, but you rarely hear this one: Nicklaus did not play golf seriously until he was 10 years old. Woods was a prodigy before he turned three. Woods cannot remember a single day in his life that was not colored, in some way, by his obsession with golf.**

sake of their children. He is very involved with his children. And the golf is not far behind. It's been difficult to maintain focus with all the off-course distractions, but I think he is firmly settled with his familial responsibilities and where his life's at now.

"Last year you saw he was a little bit more reserved. He was able to accept his failings with a little bit more humility. I think those are indicative of somebody who is in a healthy place emotionally."

Is Woods playing better because he is at peace? Or is he at peace because he is playing better? How much of his success comes from having a healthy knee, and how much is a result of a healthy outlook? There is no way to break this down mathematically: Twenty-seven percent is health, 16% is swing change, 24% is from being at peace with himself. It is all part of the picture. He can't unmix that paint.

The force that drove him from early childhood is still vibrant: Woods is still trying to conquer golf. Not professional golf or golf history. Golf. The ball at his feet and the hole in the distance. It is the constant that saved him from teenage burnout, professional

failure, and the crush of celebrity—that kept him from being golf's Jennifer Capriati, Todd Marinovich, or Lindsay Lohan. He could always retreat into the game.

That desire has brought him all the way back here, to his familiar status as the clear Masters favorite. He will arrive at Augusta facing old expectations with a new perspective.

After Woods won the WGC-Cadillac Championship earlier this month, he stood on the 18th green with his trophy as waves of PVIs (People of Varying Importance) posed for photographs with him: Finchem, Doral owner Donald Trump, Cadillac executives, Doral members, interns, assorted others.

Two Cadillacs appeared to be floating in the lake behind him. The cars were on platforms just below the surface, an old golf-tournament trick.

Woods patiently smiled and made small talk, then smiled some more, no matter who posed with him. Music blared from speakers a few hundred feet away, and between poses for the cameras he quietly bopped up and down to the beat. The child prodigy is 37 years old and looks happy. ●

TIGER WOODS

Tiger looked dominant in this seven-stroke win, which featured a round of 61 that matched his career best. But back troubles would soon derail his momentum and require surgery.

2013 WGC BRIDGESTONE

FAMILY OUTING

At the 2015 Masters Par 3 Contest, Tiger walked the course with son Charlie, daughter Sam, and girlfriend Lindsey Vonn (green dress).

2018 TOUR CHAMPIONSHIP

Woods, coming back from spinal fusion surgery in April 2017, took the Tour Championship by two strokes to earn his first win in five years.

Woods, who once conquered Augusta National with power, captured his fifth green jacket by making use of his experience.

2019 MASTERS

2019 MASTERS

Tiger, hitting at 18 on Friday, was tied for sixth after two rounds, and tied for second after three; this was his first major win in which he did not hold at least a share of the 54-hole lead.

TIGER WOODS

2019 MASTERS

Tiger drove to within three feet on
the 16th hole Sunday, and his birdie
there gave him a two-shot lead

2019 MASTERS

After his clinching putt on 18, Tiger went to his children and his mother for greenside hugs.

TIGER WOODS

2019 MASTERS

Woods, with 2018
champion Patrick
Reed, donned
the green jacket
for the first time
in 14 years.

TIGER WOODS

Excerpted from Sports Illustrated, April 22, 2019

The 2019 Masters

After all he had been through, Tiger Woods
never seemed more relatable than
when he won his 15th major

by MICHAEL ROSENBERG

On Sunday, April 7, four days before the Masters began and one day before the first official practice round, a 43-year-old father of two drove down Magnolia Lane. Some people see Augusta National Golf Club, with its power-broker members, as a locus for business, and others see it as the ultimate place of pleasure. For Tiger Woods, it is both.

Woods's friend and business partner, Rob McNamara, rode shotgun. Woods prefers to drive, and McNamara usually navigates, but Woods did not need directions. He knows the place pretty well. As he would say a few days later, he had "four coats"—Tiger-ese for green jackets. Woods and McNamara got out of their car and met up with Tiger's caddie, Joe LaCava. As the afternoon became the evening, Woods played the front nine at Augusta National the way nobody dreams of playing it.

He did not hit drives or approach shots. He just walked the front nine, and when he got near the green, he would throw a few balls down. He hit lob and sand wedges, and then he would practice his putting.

A few years ago, when Woods's back felt like it was loaded with explosives and a full golf swing could leave him writhing on the ground, this was the only kind of golf he could even try to play. Last week, it was his preference, part of a tactical mission. Woods cannot prepare for tournaments with the physical rigor he once did. But he could still prime his mind.

Augusta National favors long hitters and pure putters, but mostly it favors the wise. Woods says he has a "pretty good little library in my head of how to play the golf course," but what separates him is that he remembers where all the books are, and he knows which one to pull off the shelf. Sometimes, even when he is playing another course, he hits a shot that reminds him of one at Augusta National. This winter and early spring, he failed to win a tournament. But he believed he was hitting the shots he would need to hit to win the event that matters most to him.

As he walked those nine holes, Woods saw the angles and trajectories and spins that even some of the best players in the world can't see. He left around 7:30 p.m. The stands were empty, the course serene, and Woods was pleased. McNamara says, "He enjoyed the peaceful quiet." For a golfer who has struggled to reconcile his public and private lives, it was a well-deserved treat. That night, the course was his. Seven days later, Tiger would be ours again.

Tiger Woods won his fifth Masters, his 15th major, and his 81st PGA Tour event on Sunday, and these are astounding stats, all of them. But this is not math class, and Woods's story is not really about numbers. It is about the way he makes you feel.

You, at home, getting up early to watch a rare Sunday morning final round of three-somes, instead of twosomes, because thunderstorms would arrive in the afternoon. You, the hundreds pressed against the ropes chanting "Tiger! Tiger! Tiger!" a half hour after he had won, in a scene that was unlike any in memory here. You, whose dad took you to one of Tiger's clinics when you were a kid in Minnesota, who got you hooked on golf, and who was there Thursday, between the third green and fourth tee, catching a glimpse of Tiger again: Hello, Larry Fitzgerald. You, wearing a mint-green Under Armour golf shirt and carrying a golf umbrella Sunday morning, finding a seat near the driving range to catch a glimpse of one of the few athletes who ever dominated the way you did: Hope you got a thrill, Michael Phelps.

You, standing alongside the 11th hole Saturday afternoon…do you remember what you did? Woods hit his drive so far to the right that when caddie Joe LaCava went to look, he could not find his golfer's ball. He could also not find his golfer. In a sea of golf fans, Woods held up a driver and yelled "Joey! I'm on it right here."

Woods wiped his face with a towel and looked down at his peculiar lie. Club officials had tried to make the course walkable for spectators by pouring a kitty-litter-like substance all over the place, to soak up the rain. Woods, the golf geek, loves talking about bent grass and poa annua and Bermuda and everything in between, but he does not spend much time practicing on Tidy Cats. He carved a draw around trees and onto the green, anyway. You roared, and a few of you stopped at his divot and rubbed the cat litter with your hands.

And you, the girl and boy bouncing along under the massive oak tree outside the club-house as Woods was about to tee off Sunday, escorted by Tiger's girlfriend, Erica Herman, dressed in your daddy's trademark Sunday red and black…Sam and Charlie Woods, we know he is just your dad to you, and that's all he wants to be. But wow, have we got a story to tell you.

There was this guy called Tiger. He was supposed to win 25 majors by now. It's probably for the best that he didn't.

He was a breathtaking athlete, controlling the least controllable sport, executing shots nobody else would even try. Bobby Jones famously said Jack Nicklaus "played a game with which I am not familiar." Woods was the next evolution. He won one major by 12 strokes and another by 15. He won a U.S. Open on a broken leg and a Masters with a preposterous chip-in. He de-pantsed the whole sport.

He loved the game and we loved to watch him, and that kept us together. But he dominated so ruthlessly, and so thoroughly, that eventually we probably would have gotten tired of it. He played entire rounds without acknowledging spectators and flew through entire press conferences without saying anything memorable. He was a hard man to get to know, an even harder one to understand.

A lot has happened since then. Some of it was covered by tabloids and most of the rest can be found in his medical records. But Woods has pulled off a feat that seemed impossible when he was at his peak. He became relatable.

This is Sam and Charlie's dad now: polite, expansive, and grateful…so, so grateful. He tips his cap so often, we can draw his receding hairline from memory. He has stopped having his caddie bark at fans and started filling his rounds with small gestures. When he got in trouble on No. 17 Thursday, and a marshal asked if fans were far enough back, Woods reassured him: "Yeah, they're cool." As he walked off the 15th tee Sunday, with a chance to make history, he chatted quietly with Tony Finau, one of his playing partners. After a police officer stepped on his foot while trying to contain a crowd Friday, Woods publicly reassured him: "It's all good. Accidents happen."

Woods lets us in now. Not too far. But he lets us in. Those who see him often, in less public settings, say he is what he never was early in his career: A golfer at peace. Human interactions no longer feel transactional. Fellow players of different generations adore him. Woods followed up his Sunday night pre-Masters pitch-and-putt session by playing the back nine, tee to green, on Monday, with two of his buddies: 59-year-old Couples and 25-year-old Justin Thomas. On Wednes-

day those three played the front nine, with 35-year-old Kevin Kisner as the fourth.

It was all the preparation Woods needed. He went out the next day and shot a two-under 70, even though he didn't putt well. Storm sirens pulled him off the course on the back nine Friday, but then he caught a break. The rain stopped. He could finish Friday, saving his high-maintenance body the trouble of an early weekend double.

Woods was methodically moving up the leaderboard, one goosebump at a time. He was in the penultimate group Friday, and so every time he finished a hole, the fans left that part of the course, following him back up the hill to No. 17, and then to No. 18 and finally out the gates. It had the feel of sand falling through an hourglass. But sometimes there is more sand left than you think.

Woods said it at least three times during Masters week, but let's say it again: He did not expect to be our Tiger Woods again. When he underwent Anterior Lumbar Interbody Fusion surgery in April 2017, he wasn't even thinking about golf. He just wanted to be dad to Sam (who is now 11) and Charlie (10). He wanted to live, he says, "a normal life."

The surgery worked so well that he started playing again, and he played so well that he started believing again. With his normal life restored, he slipped back into his abnormal life.

Even when Rory McIlroy and Jordan Spieth and Brooks Koepka went on historically great runs, the biggest name on the PGA Tour was always Tiger. Now? It's Tigermania again. Minutes before Woods teed off with Ian Poulter Saturday, Poulter walked under that big oak tree toward No. 1 and nobody noticed. Then Woods walked through, the crowd erupted, and Alex Rodriguez turned his head.

Woods might seem like the same golfer he once was. He isn't. The young Tiger was so much longer than his peers that there was talk of "Tiger-proofing" courses; Sunday, Finau bombed it past him. But Woods has maintained the two qualities that separate him from just about anybody ever: His deft hands and his agile mind.

Does anybody in sports organize his thoughts like this guy? After his round on Saturday, Woods remembered exactly what the leaderboard looked like when he was on the fifth hole. He has been known to spend entire rounds locked in, blinders on, then tell a friend afterward, "I saw you on No. 4."

Three men made the short walk from the 11th green to the 12th tee on Sunday. Finau and Francesco Molinari examined their hands. Woods was counting cards. He trailed Molinari by two strokes with seven to play, but he did not think he needed to start making birdies. He knew that Brooks Koepka,

Woods knew he could bogey 18 and win—and he did so, joyously.

in the group ahead of him, had put his ball in Rae's Creek in front of the 12th green, and he figured that Koepka had hit a nine-iron toward the back-right pin, and he knew that Koepka hits it longer than he does, and so he decided he could still hit a nine-iron, but he better hit it hard and keep it left of the flag, over "the tongue of the bunker," make his par and get out of there. And that's what he did. Molinari and Finau found the creek and each made double-bogey.

Woods is such a master recovery artist that he has won majors when he drove the ball poorly. This week, most of his drives were as stress-free as the one down Magnolia Lane. He hit a perfect draw on No. 13 and made birdie. He looked up at the leaderboard, at

Koepka and Dustin Johnson and Xander Schauffele chasing him, and he channeled that old Tiger mindset: "Whatever they do, I'll just birdie the same holes. Then it's a moot point." As though making birdie were a choice anybody can just make on Sunday at the Masters.

On No. 15, Molinari found the rough, a tree, and the water to excuse himself from contention. Woods went to the library. On Thursday and Saturday, he had yelled "Get down! Get down!" at his approaches on 15, only to see them roll off the green. On Sunday, he stopped making requests and started giving orders. His shot landed on the green and stayed there, like a good little ball. Two-putt, birdie, one-stroke lead, hysteria.

At Augusta National, the only cutting-edge technology is in the golfers' bags. The course famously bans cell phones. Fans must get their news from leaderboards and their ears. It is antiquated and delightful. On Sunday, the folks around No. 17 knew that the first cheer coming from No. 16 had to be because Woods put his tee shot close, and the second cheer had to be because he sank the birdie putt to go to 14-under and take a two-stroke lead. But everybody wanted a second source. They looked up, and waited…and waited…

The leaderboard operator pulled back the row of squares next to Woods's name to insert a number and waited…and waited…and waited…waited so long, it had to be intentional. Then the row slammed shut, harder than any leaderboard row had been slammed all week, the operator's equivalent of spiking a football. There was a 14 on Woods's line, and a roar that felt straight out of 2002. Augusta National can make you feel like time stands still. Woods knows better.

Golfers compete for longer than other athletes, and so famous golfers do not just have careers and then fade from memory. They live their lives in front of us. Earl Woods, Tiger's dad, used to hold court here. He is gone now. Tida Woods, his mom, used to walk 18 holes a day, and for many years she had a tradition of walking here on Sundays with Nike founder Phil Knight. Tida walked nine holes a day last week. Some in Woods's entourage wondered if the 81-year-old Knight might show up Sunday. He did not.

The golf world hops from course to course and continent to continent, but Augusta National is where it holds reunions. Woods said he notices the same faces in the same places year after year. And then there are those he knows personally, like Amy Bartlett, Nike's global sports marketing director. She has worked with Woods for more than a decade, but the last major he won was the first she attended: The 2008 U.S. Open. Golf fans remember Woods sinking a downhill 12-foot birdie putt on the 72nd hole to force an 18-hole playoff the next day. Bartlett remembers that she didn't have a fresh red shirt for the playoff. When she sent it to be laundered at the Lodge at Torrey Pines that night, she worried it would shrink or be otherwise ruined, along with her career.

Now it's as though Woods himself came back from the laundry, looking nicer and cleaner but still like he did before.

There was no way to know that Sunday. Woods had held at least a share of the 54-hole lead in each of his first 14 major victories. This was the first time he had to come back. But that, too, was fitting. On and off the leaderboard, he no longer runs away from his peers.

He still knows how to finish, though. Woods needed a 5 on the par-4 18th and he played it so 5 was the worst score he could make. He had spent the afternoon adding to his library: "I hit some of the best shots on that back nine today. You know, I felt like I just flushed it coming home, which was a nice feeling."

He had won this tournament first as a son and now as a father. He had gone from phenom to cyborg to the man he wanted to be.

Woods was on 17 when Sam and Charlie emerged from the clubhouse. They are not like their dad: When they go to Augusta National, they need McNamara to show them around. They had never been there before. They tried to head left. McNamara said, "This way!" and took them to the right, where they finally just climbed over a chain and down a path, and they stood just behind the TV towers on 18, waiting for Daddy to get off work. Woods—who once said his ideal foursome would just be a twosome, him and his dad—putted out for his Masters-sealing 5, ripped a double-fist pump, and hugged Tida and Sam and Charlie.

Several young PGA Tour stars watched the finish in the clubhouse. They grew up watching Tiger win majors, then they got to know him, and on Sunday they combined the experiences. In a bar in the clubhouse, Justin Thomas sat with family and friends; Thomas had made a hole-in-one on No. 16 Sunday, so he bought a round of drinks. Thomas was asked about the practice rounds with Tiger. Nothing stood out as unusual, except for who was playing, and where.

"I'm not surprised he won," Thomas said. "He always plays well here."

When Woods emerged after signing his scorecard, Thomas, Koepka, Bubba Watson, Rickie Fowler, Zach Johnson, and Mike Weir were among those who greeted him. This is not a normal scene. But this was not a normal week. Twenty-two years ago, Woods had signed a flag here TO FLUFF, THE NO. 1 CADDIE IN THE WORLD. This time, LaCava walked out carrying a flagstick. He has now won the Masters with three different caddies. He could probably win without one.

Herman told Koepka's mother, Denise Jakows, "your son almost gave me a heart attack."

Woods told Watson, "I'm not crying yet."

"You will be," Watson said.

He had a second red shirt that he didn't need, and a fifth green coat that he also didn't need but will happily wear. There was, as you might expect, more math: Questions about whether Tiger can break Nicklaus's record of 18 majors. And naturally, there were comparisons to Ben Hogan's comeback from a car wreck and broken bones, and Nicklaus's stunning win in 1986, at age 46.

Those are just discussion topics, though. They are not his story. It doesn't matter if Woods's win is bigger than Nicklaus's or if his comeback is better than Hogan's. He seems to understand that implicitly.

Around 4 p.m., most of Woods's closest supporters climbed in a pair of Mercedes SUVs in the champions' parking lot. Some of what filled the cars would have looked familiar to a 21-year-old Woods (clubs, suitcase, flagstick) and some would not (his launch monitor, Sam, Charlie.)

Rain fell gently on Augusta National. How much time had passed? Seven days, 14 years, a lifetime. This is where he took ownership of the sport, in 1997, and where he completed the Tiger Slam, in 2001. It is where his ailing father Earl watched him win in 2005—the old man flew to Georgia against his doctors' wishes. He died 13 months later. This is where former Augusta National chairman Billy Payne lectured him in public after his infidelities, and where he felt safe returning to competitive golf anyway. And now it is where he hugged Sam and Charlie after his 15th major, and where they finally got to witness the hold this game has on their pops, and the hold he has on the rest of us. ●

ZOZO CHAMPIONSHIP

FedEx

RECORD-TYING
82 PGA TOUR WINS

Tiger posed with tournament volunteers after capturing the Zozo Championshp—the first Tour event ever held in Japan—in October 2019 and tying Sam Snead's record of 82 Tour wins.

FATHER AND SON

Tiger Woods and Charlie, 11, teamed up at the PNC Championship, a father-son event in Orlando, in December 2020.

Front Man

From his pro debut year of 1996 to his
Masters comeback in 2019, Tiger Woods has appeared
on the cover of SI 22 times

December 23, 1996

October 28, 1996

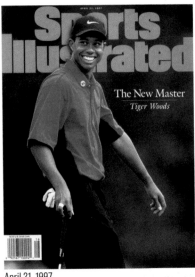

April 21, 1997

October 6, 1997

December 18, 2000

April 13, 1998

August 23, 1999

April 3, 2000

June 26, 2000

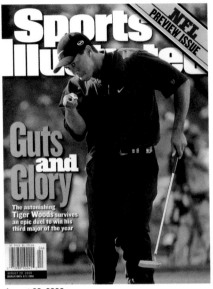

August 28, 2000

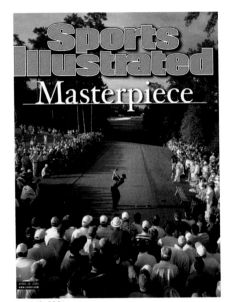

April 16, 2001

July 25, 2005

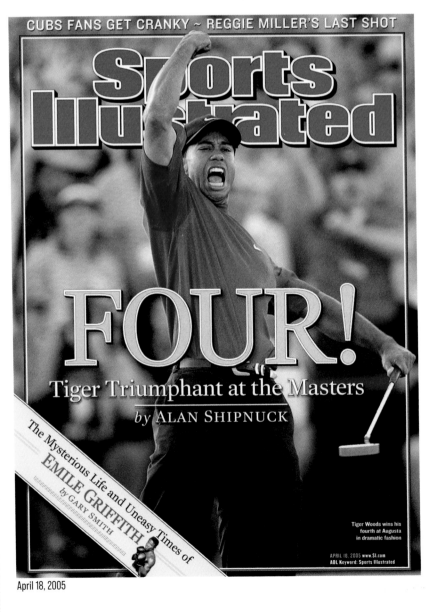

April 18, 2005

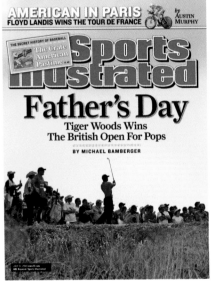

July 31, 2006

April 2, 2007

April 16, 2007

March 2, 2009

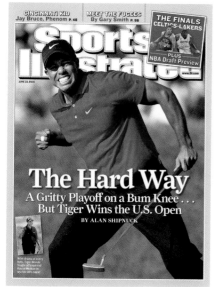
June 23, 2008

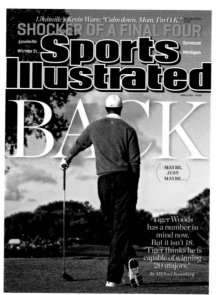
April 8, 2013

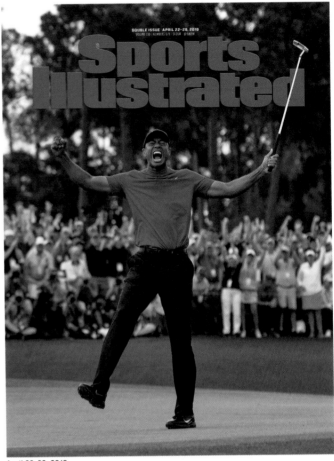

April 4, 2016

April 22–29, 2019

Photo Credits

Cover: Fred Vuich **Back Cover:** John Biever **Interior:** Page 1: Simon Bruty; Page 2: Robert Beck; Page 6: David Liam Kyle; Page 7: Al Tielemans; Page 10: John Burgess; Page 12: CBS Photo Archive; Page 13: CBS Photo Archive; Page 14: V.J. Lovero; Page 16: Michael O'Bryon; Page 22: Peter Read Miller; Page 26: Jacqueline Duvoisin; Page 28: Robert Beck; Page 40: John Iacono; Page 42: Robert Beck; Page 44: Heinz Kluetmeier; Page 50: Robert Beck; Page 52: Craig Jones/Allsport; Page 54: Paul Sancya/AP Photo; Page 55: Michael Conroy/AP Photo; Page 56: Bob Martin; Page 66: Robert Beck; Page 68: Robert Beck; Page 70: John Burgess; Page 73: Simon Bruty; Page 76: Bob Martin; Page 78: Robert Beck; Page 79: Sam Miller/AP Photo; Page 80: Adam Butler/AP Photo; Page 81: Robert Beck; Page 84: Adam Butler/AP Photo; Page 86: Robert Beck; Page 88: Bob Rosato; Page 90: Charlie Neibergall/AP Photo; Page 91: John Biever; Page 93: Ed Reinke/AP Photo; Page 100: Fred Vuich; Page 102: Robert Beck; Page 104: Robert Beck; Page 108: Robert Beck; Page 112: Al Tielemans; Page 114: Simon Bruty; Page 116: Simon Bruty; Page 117: Al Tielemans; Page 118: Fred Vuich; Page 120: Al Tielemans; Page 121: Bob Martin; Page 122: Bob Martin; Page 124: John W. McDonough; Page 126: Neil Leifer; Page 128: Robert Beck; Page 130: Al Tielemans; Page 131: Neil Leifer; Page 132: John Biever; Page 138: John Biever; Page 140: Fred Vuich; Page 142: Robert Beck; Page 144: Fred Vuich; Page 146: Fred Vuich; Page 147: Robert Beck; Page 148: John Biever; Page 150: John Biever; Page 151: John Biever; Page 156: John Biever; Page 158: Darren Carroll; Page 160: Fred Vuich; Page 161: Robert Beck; Page 162: Robert Beck; Page 164: Fred Vuich; Page 166: John Biever; Page 168: Robert Beck; Page 170: Fred Vuich; Page 172: Fred Vuich; Page 174: Al Tielemans; Page 175: Robyn Beck/AFP; Page 176: Robert Beck; Page 178: Fred Vuich; Page 182: John Biever; Page 186: Eric Gay/AP Photo; Page 189: Lori Moffett/AP Photo; Page 190: Fred Vuich; Page 192: Fred Vuich; Page 202: Thomas Anderson/AFLO; Page 204: Robert Beck; Page 206: John Amis/AP Photo; Page 208: Kohjiro Kinno; Page 210: Kohjiro Kinno; Page 212: Kohjiro Kinno; Page 214: Al Tielemans; Page 215: Al Tielemans; Page 216: Kohjiro Kinno; Page 221: Kohjiro Kinno; Page 224: Lee Jin-man/AP Photo; Page 226: Phelan M. Ebenhack/AP Photo

Library of Congress Cataloging-in-Publication Data available upon request.

This book is available in quantity at special discounts for your group or organization. For further information, contact:

Triumph Books LLC
814 North Franklin Street
Chicago, Illinois 60610
(312) 337-0747
www.triumphbooks.com

Printed in U.S.A.
ISBN: 978-1-62937-946-3